Pairwork and Groupwork

Multi-level photocopiable activities for teenagers

Meredith Levy
Nicholas Murgatroyd

CAMBRIDGE
UNIVERSITY PRESS

CAMBRIDGE UNIVERSITY PRESS
Cambridge, New York, Melbourne, Madrid, Cape Town,
Singapore, São Paulo, Delhi, Mexico City

Cambridge University Press
The Edinburgh Building, Cambridge CB2 8RU, UK

www.cambridge.org
Information on this title: www.cambridge.org/9780521716338

First published 2009
4th printing 2012

Printed in Poland by Opolgraf

A catalogue record for this publication is available from the British Library

ISBN 978-0-521-71633-8 Book

Contents

Map of the book

P = pairwork
G = groupwork
C = whole class

	Title	Level	Language focus	Skills focus	Activity type
1 Personal information	1.1 Meet the new me	elementary	present simple, *have got*, personal information questions	speaking: asking for and giving personal information	role card game (P)
	1.2 Me, conditionally	intermediate	second conditional	speaking: talking about imagined possibilities	board game (G)
	1.3 Knowing me	upper-intermediate	present simple, *like/ enjoy + -ing*, *would like*, second conditional	speaking: answering questions about yourself	prompt cards for speaking (G)
2 The family	2.1 We are family	elementary	present simple questions	speaking: defining words for members of the family	information-gap crossword (G, P)
	2.2 Families large and small	intermediate	present simple, *would*, *should*, comparative and superlative adjectives	reading and speaking: making comparisons, giving advice, expressing opinions	discussion (P, G)
	2.3 My roots	upper-intermediate	idioms; language of opinions	speaking: talking about families and relationships	questionnaire and discussion (P, G)
3 Daily activities	3.1 Their day, your day, my day	elementary	time; present simple questions	speaking: exchanging information about routines	information-gap clocks (P)
	3.2 Your week	intermediate	present simple, present continuous; expressions of frequency	speaking: asking about daily routines and future plans	survey with whole class mingle (C, P)
	3.3 Board of life	upper-intermediate	questions with *how often*; expressions of frequency	speaking: talking about lifestyles; follow-up questions	board game (G)
4 Homes	4.1 What's different?	elementary	*there is/are*; prepositions of place	speaking: describing the location of objects	spot the difference (P)
	4.2 My home	intermediate	present simple, *would*, second conditional, comparative and superlative adjectives	speaking: talking at length about homes and neighbourhoods; follow-up questions	prompt cards for speaking (G)
	4.3 My area	upper-intermediate	language of opinions; connectors	speaking: expressing opinions about neighbourhoods; justifying decisions	ranking activity and discussion (P, G)

Map of the book

	Title	Level	Language focus	Skills focus	Activity type
5 Getting around	5.1 In town	elementary	prepositions; present simple	reading and speaking: describing location; giving directions	information-gap map (P)
	5.2 The way to go	intermediate	mixed tenses	writing and speaking: asking questions about transport and travel	survey with whole class mingle (G, C)
	5.3 Around the world in 25 days	upper-intermediate	language of suggestions; future with *will* and *going to*	speaking: making plans; expressing opinions; giving a presentation	planning a trip (G)
6 Customs and traditions	6.1 Our birthdays	elementary	dates; *in* + month; *on* + date; possessive *'s*	speaking: asking for and giving dates	survey with whole class mingle (C, P)
	6.2 Festivals quiz	intermediate	*Wh-* questions; dates	reading and speaking: discussing and answering quiz questions	quiz (G)
	6.3 A new festival	upper-intermediate	past, present and future tenses	writing and speaking: organising information; note taking; giving a presentation	presentation (G)
7 Food and drink	7.1 Eating habits	elementary	present and past simple questions; expressions of frequency	speaking: asking for and giving information about eating habits	survey with whole class mingle (C, P)
	7.2 Who's coming to dinner?	intermediate	*going to* for plans, *will* for predictions; prepositions of place	speaking: planning a function; expressing opinions; making predictions; giving a presentation	planning a dinner party (P)
	7.3 Healthy eating	upper-intermediate	present simple; *should*	writing and speaking: categorising and making lists; discussing eating habits	filling in tables (P)
8 Descriptions	8.1 What can you see?	elementary	present continuous questions and statements; *have got*	speaking: describing actions and clothing	spot the difference (P)
	8.2 What can it describe?	intermediate	adjectives	writing and speaking: defining adjectives	information-gap crossword (P)
	8.3 Guess what it is	upper-intermediate	present simple; present simple passive	speaking: explaining what things are and what they are used for	picture card guessing game (G)
9 Friends	9.1 My perfect friend	elementary	present simple statements; *and, but, because*	writing and speaking: expressing opinions; describing a friend	questionnaire and writing a poem (P)
	9.2 The best of friends	intermediate	present simple; present perfect; *should*	speaking: discussing friendship; giving advice	questionnaire and problem page letters (P, G)
	9.3 Friendship	upper-intermediate	question forms (present simple, present perfect, second conditional)	writing and speaking: creating and conducting a survey; summarising information	creating a survey (G, C)

Map of the book

	Title	Level	Language focus	Skills focus	Activity type
10 The natural world	10.1 Nature game	elementary	adjectives; present simple; *can*, *have got*	speaking: describing features of the natural world	board game (G)
	10.2 Quick descriptions	intermediate	present simple; adjectives	speaking: describing appearance, characteristics and habits	guessing game with cards (G)
	10.3 The power of nature	upper-intermediate	present simple; present passive	writing and speaking: describing characteristics; making factual explanations	information-gap crossword (P)
11 Education	11.1 Our ideal timetable	elementary	time; *on* + day; *at* + time	speaking: talking about activities on a timetable; expressing opinions	planning a timetable (P)
	11.2 Finish the sentence	intermediate	modals: *should*, *must*, *ought to*, *have to*; verb + infinitive with *to*	reading and speaking: forming sentences; giving reasons for opinions	matching card game (G)
	11.3 Leaving school	upper-intermediate	mixed tenses; modals	speaking: expressing opinions; agreeing and disagreeing	role play (G)
12 Leisure time	12.1 World of sport	elementary	present simple; gerunds	speaking: asking and answering questions about sports	memory card game (G)
	12.2 Music and me	intermediate	present simple questions; gerunds	writing and speaking: completing a questionnaire; expressing opinions	questionnaire and discussion (P, G)
	12.3 Life of leisure	upper-intermediate	language of opinions	speaking: talking at length about leisure time; arguing a point	prompt cards for speaking (G)
13 Fame	13.1 Press conference	elementary	present simple; past simple; present continuous; *going to*	writing and speaking: creating a profile; doing an interview	role play interviews (G)
	13.2 Monroe and Chaplin	intermediate	past simple; past simple passive; past continuous	reading and speaking: scanning a text for information; asking questions	information-gap reading (P)
	13.3 Hall of fame	upper-intermediate	*should*; mixed tenses; comparative and superlative adjectives	writing and speaking: expressing opinions and giving reasons	discussion and written explanation (G)

	Title	Level	Language focus	Skills focus	Activity type
14 Jobs	14.1 Guess my job	elementary	present simple questions	speaking: asking for information; making deductions	guessing game with cards (G)
	14.2 Job interviews	intermediate	mixed tenses	reading and speaking: responding to a job advert; doing a job interview	role play interviews (P, G)
	14.3 My ideal job	upper-intermediate	present simple questions; gerunds; *would*	writing and speaking: completing a questionnaire; identifying personal attributes and skills	guessing game and questionnaire (P)
15 The past	15.1 Past history	elementary	*Wh-* questions; past simple	reading and speaking: answering quiz questions	quiz card game (G)
	15.2 School reunion	intermediate	past simple; present perfect; present continuous	reading and speaking: describing past events and experiences; describing present activities	role card game (G or C)
	15.3 Mixed stories	upper-intermediate	past simple; past continuous; past perfect	reading and speaking: sequencing two stories; devising endings	scrambled stories (P)
16 The world around us	16.1 What are you doing?	elementary	*is/are*; present continuous	speaking: talking on the phone; describing places and present activities	picture-based phone calls (P)
	16.2 Ask the question	intermediate	*Wh-* questions; mixed tenses	speaking: asking questions	questions to elicit specific answers (P)
	16.3 Amazon	upper-intermediate	modals; *can, should, must*; first conditional; *to* + infinitive of purpose	speaking: stating opinions, giving reasons, negotiating	planning an adventure (G)
17 The future	17.1 Plans and predictions	elementary	*will* for predictions; *going to* for plans	speaking: asking and answering questions about the future	survey with whole class mingle (G, C)
	17.2 Life changes	intermediate	*will* and *going to* for predictions	writing and speaking: describing events and situations in the future	picture-based stories (P)
	17.3 Things to come	upper-intermediate	*will, might*; future perfect; future passive	speaking: predicting and speculating about the future	picture-based discussion (G)

Introduction

What is *Pairwork and Groupwork*?

Pairwork and Groupwork is a photocopiable resource book designed to give teenage students the opportunity to communicate with one another in English in meaningful and enjoyable ways.

Who is *Pairwork and Groupwork* for?

Pairwork and Groupwork is for teachers of English who want to provide their students with stimulating communication activities for pairs and groups. The activities have been primarily designed for use with learners aged between 11 and 16, though many activities can also be successfully used with older classes. While the activities are designed to reinforce and supplement coursebook material, teenage students should find them interesting and fun to do in their own right. The activities are clear and simple to use, with minimal preparation required.

How is *Pairwork and Groupwork* organised?

Pairwork and Groupwork is divided into 17 units, each focusing on a different topic of interest to teenagers. Each unit provides one activity for the following levels – elementary, intermediate and upper-intermediate – although this division is not rigid and activities may be used with students of a different level. The Map of the book and the summary panels for the activities give information on which lexical, grammatical and skill areas are covered. This allows easy integration into your syllabus. The Map of the book also tells you whether each activity is primarily for pairwork, groupwork or the whole class. Each activity is accompanied by clear, step-by-step instructions, as well as an indication of how much preparation and class time is needed.

What type of activities are in *Pairwork and Groupwork*?

In all activities, students work independently in pairs or groups and are encouraged to communicate naturally and spontaneously to complete the tasks. Some activities involve a mixture of pairwork and groupwork. All have a major focus on speaking and listening, and in many cases also call on reading and writing skills. Many of the activities involve information-gap tasks which will keep students motivated and engaged. Activity types include board and card games, role plays, quizzes, surveys, problem-solving activities, story-telling and group presentations.

How is each activity organised?

The teacher's notes for each activity provide a warm-up task to lead in to the main activity and several suggestions for follow-ups. The main activity is explained clearly and simply in numbered steps. However, the lesson plans are flexible and can easily be adapted to what best suits your students, your teaching style and the context.

How can I get the most out of *Pairwork and Groupwork*?

Preparation

Some warm-up activities can be more stimulating if you are able to bring in pictures, photos or maps. However, for most activities, preparation before the class only involves photocopying the activity page and possibly cutting it into separate cards or sections. If you have time, it's a good idea to laminate these or back them with cardboard so that they are more durable and can be reused. In the case of card games, you may like to enlarge the cards when you are photocopying.

For board games, a tossed coin can be used instead of dice to determine how many spaces students move around the board. Coins can also be used in place of counters. Rules for games are set out in boxes in the teacher's notes – if you wish, you can photocopy these and hand them out for students to refer to while they are playing the game.

Timing

The summary panel for each activity in the teacher's notes suggests a time for the warm-up and the main activity. However, this is only an estimate – timing will vary according to the size and ability of your class. If some pairs or groups finish an activity early, ask them to go round and help others who are working more slowly.

Vocabulary and grammar

A variable amount of time at the warm-up stage may be needed to either pre-teach or revise vocabulary or grammatical structures – the summary panel lists words and structures that are required for the activity. For upper-intermediate activities the range of vocabulary is broader and generally more open to students' own choice.

Managing the main activity

We suggest that you vary the composition of pairs and groups so that students work with a variety of different people. For some activities, it may be a good idea to put together students who don't know each other very well, while for others you may decide to put students into friendship groups. You may like to pair up weak and strong students or students of similar levels for certain activities.

If your class doesn't divide neatly into pairs or into groups of the recommended number, the activities can often be adjusted so that two students work together as one. Alternatively, the extra student(s) can be asked to help you monitor the activity or you can join in the activity yourself to make up the numbers.

Ensure that students fully understand what they are to do before they start working in their pairs or groups. In monolingual classes, you may find it worthwhile to explain the task in the students' own language, to save time and avoid confusion. Announce time limits for the activities at the outset, but be prepared to be flexible.

While pairs/groups are working on the activity, go round to listen, give help if needed and settle any disagreements. Avoid intervening to correct students' language unless there is an actual problem of communication – remember that the main emphasis of these activities is on fluency and success in communicating rather than on strict accuracy. You can make a note of common errors and address them later. Try also to make a note of language that students are using effectively.

Follow-up

The follow-up suggestions are optional – you can use or adapt them as appropriate, depending on the students' interest and the time you have available. Some are designed for classroom use, either to round off the lesson or to build on the main activity in a follow-up lesson. Others offer interesting ideas for homework tasks, often involving the use of the Internet as a language resource. Tasks suitable for homework include writing a variety of text types, researching topics of interest, doing projects, designing posters and preparing presentations.

Finally, remember that the process is just as important as the end product. We hope that both you and your students will enjoy working with *Pairwork and Groupwork*.

Meet the new me

Language focus
present simple, *have got*;
personal information
questions

Key vocabulary
favourite possession;
personal information

Skills focus
speaking: asking for
and giving personal
information

Level
elementary

Time
30 minutes

Preparation
one photocopy for each
pair, cut into 4 separate
cards; each student will
need 2 cards

Warm-up

❶ Write the phrase *favourite possession* on the board and explain it using examples such as *My favourite possession is my new car; Tom's favourite possession is his mobile phone.* Ask a few students what their favourite possession is.

❷ Invite a student to the front and interview him/her using the prompts from the identity card on the worksheet, starting with *What's your name?* Then ask students to ask you similar personal information questions.

❸ Now take on a new identity by putting the name of a famous person on the board or showing them a picture of someone famous. Explain that this is *the new me*. Ask them to question you again, this time answering as if you were that person. Help them with the question formation.

Main activity

❶ Hand out an identity card to each student. Tell them that they have to write on the card to create a new identity for themselves. Explain that this person will be *the new me*. They cannot put any information on the card that is true about themselves now. Their new identity could be someone famous, someone else in the school, a relative or an imaginary person. If they wish, they can draw a picture of themselves in the 'photo' area. Make sure students work individually.

❷ Elicit the questions necessary for students to gain personal information from their classmates, using the prompts on the card. Possible questions they could use are:
What's your name? How old are you? What do you do?
Where are you from? Where do you live? What do you like?
Have you got any brothers or sisters? Have you got any pets?
What's your favourite possession?

❸ Ask students to interview each other in pairs. Stress that they cannot write down their partner's answers but should try to remember as much information as possible.

❹ Now give each student a new blank identity card. Put them into new pairs, well away from their original partners.

❺ Explain that they have to interview their new partner about his/her original partner and write the answers on the new card. They will need to use questions like *What's his name? How old is she?* If necessary, revise the third person form of the questions.

❻ Tell students to exchange cards so that they each have a completed card with information about their original partner on it. They then return to their original partner. They each compare the card written about them with the original card that they wrote themselves. Ask them how much information was communicated correctly.

Follow-up

○ Give each student another blank identity card but with the name of a celebrity filled in. Ask them to use websites to complete the other details. They can then read out the details and ask other students to guess who the celebrity is.

○ Ask students to write a paragraph entitled *The new me*, using their new identity.

Name: ....

Age: ....

Job: ....

From: ....

Live: ....

Like: ....

....

Brothers/sisters: ....

....

Pets: ....

Favourite possession: ....

....

Name: ....

Age: ....

Job: ....

From: ....

Live: ....

Like: ....

....

Brothers/sisters: ....

....

Pets: ....

Favourite possession: ....

....

Name: ....

Age: ....

Job: ....

From: ....

Live: ....

Like: ....

....

Brothers/sisters: ....

....

Pets: ....

Favourite possession: ....

....

Name: ....

Age: ....

Job: ....

From: ....

Live: ....

Like: ....

....

Brothers/sisters: ....

....

Pets: ....

Favourite possession: ....

....

Me, conditionally

Language focus
second conditional

Key vocabulary
ambition, celebrate, counter, heads, hobby, move forward, possession, relax, spy, start, surf the net, tails, toss a coin

Skills focus
speaking: talking about imagined possibilities

Level
intermediate

Time
40 minutes

Preparation
one photocopy for each group of 3 or 4 students; a coin for each group and a counter for each student; a photocopy of the Rules for each group (optional)

Warm-up

❶ Ask students a few personal questions such as *What are you afraid of?* When you have asked students a question, ask them to transform it so that it becomes part of a second conditional question, e.g. *What would you be afraid of if you were two?* Use the phrases on the worksheet to help you.

❷ Introduce the language of board games from the key vocabulary.

Main activity

❶ Divide the students into groups of three or four. Hand out a copy of the board to each group. You may also want to hand out a copy of the Rules. Make sure each group has a coin and knows which side is 'heads' and which is 'tails'. Each student will also need something he/she can use as a counter.

❷ Explain the rules for this activity (see the Rules box below). When a student lands on a square, he/she must form a question for the person sitting on their right. The question should be in the second conditional and must end with one of the phrases from the centre of the board. When a student lands on a square with a letter, they have an extra turn. The first student to return to the square they started from is the winner.

❸ If necessary, help with vocabulary and resolve debates about the questions. The students should try and choose phrases that work well. They should have fun with the questions and answers rather than expecting all of them to make sense.

Follow-up

⭕ Ask students to write a week's diary entry, imagining their life in a different situation. They could, for example, write a diary of how their life would be if they were 60, lived in Australia, or had a lot of money.

⭕ In pairs, students write five new questions using the second conditional. They can try them out with another pair.

Rules for Me, conditionally

1 Place a counter for each player on a square with a letter.

2 Take it in turns to toss the coin.

3 If it is 'heads', move forward one square.

4 If it is 'tails', move forward two squares.

5 When you land on a square, make a question using the words and one of the phrases in the middle of the board. Ask the player sitting on your right your question. For example: *If you were 20, how would you celebrate your birthday?*

6 He/she must answer your question.

7 When it is your turn you must not ask a question that another player has asked before.

8 When you land on a square with a letter, toss the coin again and have another turn.

9 The first player to return to the square they started from is the winner.

From *Pairwork and Groupwork* © Cambridge University Press 2009 **PHOTOCOPIABLE**

1.2 Me, conditionally

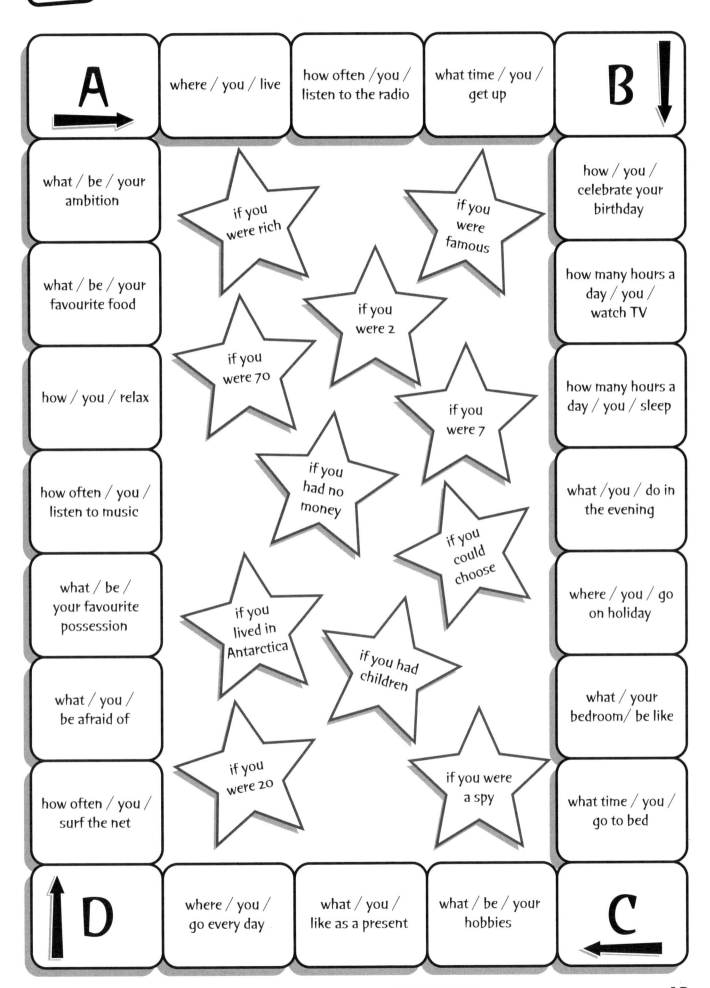

A →

where / you / live

how often / you / listen to the radio

what time / you / get up

B ↓

what / be / your ambition

if you were rich

if you were famous

how / you / celebrate your birthday

what / be / your favourite food

if you were 2

how many hours a day / you / watch TV

how / you / relax

if you were 70

if you were 7

how many hours a day / you / sleep

how often / you / listen to music

if you had no money

what / you / do in the evening

what / be / your favourite possession

if you could choose

where / you / go on holiday

if you lived in Antarctica

if you had children

what / you / be afraid of

what / your bedroom / be like

if you were 20

if you were a spy

how often / you / surf the net

what time / you / go to bed

D ↑

where / you / go every day

what / you / like as a present

what / be / your hobbies

C ←

Knowing me

Language focus
present simple; *like/enjoy + -ing*; *would like*; second conditional

Key vocabulary
ambition, fear, memory, personality, pessimist, possession, proud

Skills focus
speaking: answering questions about yourself

Level
upper-intermediate

Time
30 minutes

Preparation
one photocopy for each group of 3 or 4 students, cut into separate cards

Extra notes
This activity is particularly useful to break the ice for new classes. It is also useful for speaking exam practice.

Warm-up

❶ Ask students what they know about the person sitting next to them. Use questions like these to elicit the information:
What is he good at?
What kind of food does she like?
What does he do in his free time?
What does she want to be?
How many brothers and sisters has he got?

❷ Extend this activity by using the key vocabulary in the panel to ask further questions. Put the words on the board if necessary.

Main activity

❶ Divide the class into groups of three or four. Give each group a set of cards placed face down in the middle of the table.

❷ Ask a student to take a card and ask you the question on it. Answer the question about yourself as an example. Aim to speak for about half a minute. Then ask a student the same question. Encourage students to ask follow-up questions.

❸ Explain to students that they should take it in turns to take a card and ask the person on their right to answer it. That person should aim to speak for about half a minute. When the student has finished speaking, the other students should ask follow-up questions. The card should then be returned to the bottom of the pile.

❹ Complete the activity with the whole class by asking each student to tell you something interesting they discovered about someone in their group.

Follow-up

○ Ask students to write a list with the title *Five things you didn't know about me* but without adding their name. Collect them in and read out one or two lists, asking the class to guess is the identity of the student. Put the other lists on the wall so the students can move around reading them and trying to identify whose they are.

○ Ask students to write a short essay in answer to one of the questions on the cards. This can be a question of their choice or one they draw randomly from the pack of question cards.

What do you think is your best quality?

What would you most like to change about your personality?

Who do you most enjoy spending time with?

What's your ambition?

What's your greatest fear?

What makes you happy?

What are you most proud of?

Where would you like to live in the future?

What's your favourite possession?

What do you like doing at the weekend?

What's your earliest memory?

Are you an optimist or a pessimist?

What's your favourite way to travel?

What's the most interesting thing about your family?

If you could go anywhere, where would you go and what would you do?

What makes you sad?

How different would your life be without the Internet?

If you could meet someone famous, who would you choose?

We are family

Language focus
present simple questions

Key vocabulary
families and
relatives; *granddad,
granddaughter,
grandma, grandson,
nephew, niece*

Skills focus
speaking: defining words
for members of the
family

Level
elementary

Time
30 minutes

Preparation
one photocopy for each
pair, cut into A and B
parts

Extra notes
Dictionaries may be
useful for this activity.

Warm-up

❶ Introduce the topic of 'family' by putting the following anagrams on the board and asking students to solve them in pairs: *hareft, ohmert, yamfil* (father, mother, family).

❷ Ask students to come up with a way of describing *mother* and/or *father* without saying the actual word, e.g. *I am this man's son/daughter.*

Main activity

❶ Tell students they are going to complete a crossword puzzle but will have to do some preparation first. Divide the class into two halves, one on each side of the room.

❷ Give one half of the class an A worksheet each and the other half a B worksheet each. Ask them to look at all the words on their part of the puzzle and check that they know what they mean.

❸ In pairs or small groups, they decide how they are going to explain the words to the others, without saying the actual words. You may want to give out dictionaries.

❹ When students are confident that they understand the words and can describe them, reorganise the class. Put each student from the A half with a student from the B half so that each pair has two versions of the puzzle.

❺ Students take it in turns to ask for definitions (e.g. *What's 6 down? What's 3 across?*) and fill in the missing words. They must not look at their partner's worksheet. If they are having problems guessing the word, their partner helps them by saying the first letter, then the second letter.

❻ When they have finished, students compare puzzles and find out if they have the correct answers.

❼ In pairs, they look at the prompts below the puzzle. They use the prompts to ask each other the questions.

Answers
How many brothers or sisters have you got?
How many cousins have you got?
How old is your youngest relative?
Who is your favourite relative? Why?

❽ Finally, find out who has the most cousins or the most brothers and sisters in the class.

Follow-up

○ In pairs, ask students to write the words under the headings *girls/women* and *boys/men*. Then they play a game where one student says a family word and the other student has to give the masculine/feminine equivalent.

○ Ask students to write a short descriptive paragraph about their own family or their favourite family member, using plenty of adjectives.

○ In another lesson, students bring in photos of members of their extended families. The others have to guess how they are related – whether they are an *uncle/father, aunt/mother*, etc.

A

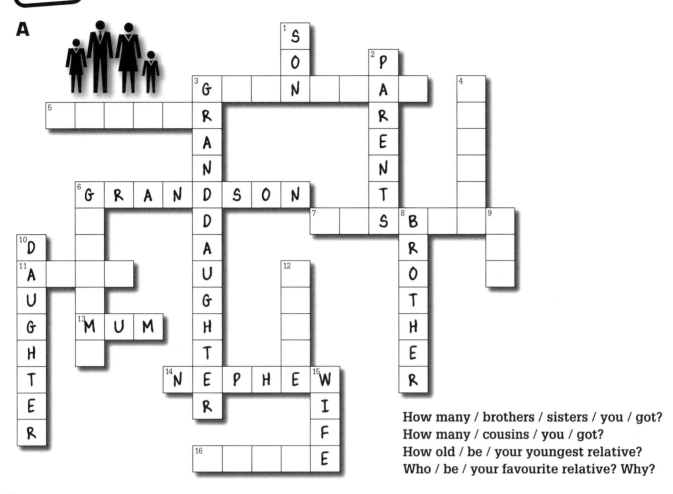

How many / brothers / sisters / you / got?
How many / cousins / you / got?
How old / be / your youngest relative?
Who / be / your favourite relative? Why?

B

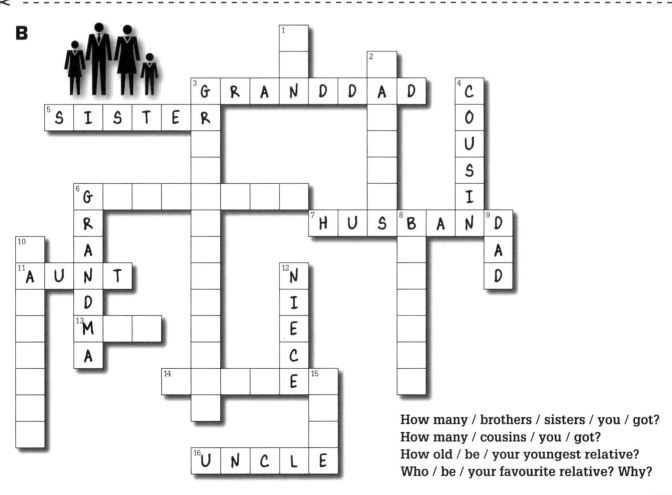

How many / brothers / sisters / you / got?
How many / cousins / you / got?
How old / be / your youngest relative?
Who / be / your favourite relative? Why?

Families large and small

Language focus
present simple; *would, should*; comparative and superlative adjectives

Key vocabulary
easy-going, ideal, improve, on your own, only child, relationship, secure, share, similar, treat

Skills focus
reading and speaking: making comparisons; giving advice; expressing opinions

Level
intermediate

Time
45 minutes

Preparation
one photocopy for each student

Extra notes
If possible, bring in some of your own family photos for the Warm-up.

Warm-up

❶ Describe your own family and childhood. Talk about whether you had any brothers or sisters or were an only child. Show them your family photos if you have them.

❷ Ask one or two students about their own families. Use these questions to introduce the key vocabulary: *What's the ideal number of sisters? Do you have a good relationship with your brother? Are you an easy-going person? Do you feel secure when you are with your family?*

Main activity

❶ Divide the class into pairs and hand out a worksheet to each student. Ask them to look at the first set of questions. Explain that they have to ask each other these questions and discuss the answers. After a few minutes, develop this as a whole class discussion.

❷ Now ask students to put their worksheets face down on their desks. Tell students that they are going to read about two teenagers and what they say about their families. Explain that one of them is an only child and the other is from a larger family.

❸ In pairs, they predict what the teenagers might say about their experience of growing up.

❹ When they are ready, they then turn over their worksheets, read the texts and find out if any of their predictions were correct.

❺ Now tell them to look at the questions below the texts and discuss their answers in pairs. They should justify their opinions and suggest useful advice for Michelle and Jack. Follow this up by inviting them to share their suggestions with the rest of the class.

❻ Reorganise students into groups of three or four and ask them to discuss the questions in the final section.

Follow-up

○ Ask students to write an essay describing their own family and how they feel about it.

○ Students write two lists outlining the advantages and disadvantages of small and large families. If they need help, possible suggestions are:

Small family	Large family
Parents have more time for you .	*There are other children to play with.*
It's quiet at home for doing homework.	*It's more fun.*
You always get new things, not second-hand things.	*You can look after each other.*
You don't have to argue over the TV or computer.	*Brothers and sisters can help each other with homework.*
You can decide what to do in your free time.	*You can borrow clothes, CDs and other things.*
You can spend time alone.	*You are never lonely.*
You don't have to share.	*You learn how to share.*

1 Work with a partner and discuss these questions.
1 How many people are there in your family?
2 What do you think is the ideal number of people in a family?
3 Are families in your country today getting bigger or smaller?
4 What do you think is the best age to become a parent?
5 Do you think being close in age is the most important thing in relationships between members of a family? Why? / Why not?

2 Read the texts below about Michelle and Jack. Then answer the questions.

Michelle

I don't live near many of my friends from school, so I spend a lot of my free time at home. I know that some people think that being an only child can be lonely, but I don't think it's a problem. I have the Internet at home and, of course, a mobile phone, so it's very easy to contact my friends. And both my parents are really easy-going and cool to spend time with. For example, they both love playing computer games, so we have family competitions. And we often go cycling together when the weather's good.

I've got a lot of cousins and it's great in the holidays when we get together, but I like being on my own sometimes. I don't know how I'd feel if I always had to share everything with a brother or sister.

I've got two older brothers, but there's a big difference in age between us. One brother is ten years older than me and the other one's eight years older. When I was younger, I used to love having older brothers, it made me feel very secure. They always took me to the park and other places when my parents were busy. It's not so good now though. They've both left home, and when they come to visit, they treat me like a child. I think they forget that I'm growing up too.

A lot of the time it's just me and my parents, so it's a bit like being an only child. Mum and Dad try to spend time with me, but they're both very busy. A lot of the time I'm at home on my own. I've got the Internet and plenty of great things. But sometimes I wish I had someone my age to spend time with, especially when we go on holiday.

Jack

1 Who do you think has a better life at home?
2 What advice would you give to Michelle or Jack to improve their lives at home?
3 Are either of their situations similar to or different from yours?

3 Work in a group. Discuss these questions.
1 How much time do you spend with your mother or father?
2 What do you do together?
3 Do you have any brothers or sisters?
4 How different do you think your life would be with/without them?
5 Would you like to have children one day? Why? / Why not?

My roots

Language focus
idioms; language of opinions

Key vocabulary
black sheep, bring up (children), extended family, generation (gap), intelligence, previous, run in (a family), take after, talent

Skills focus
speaking: talking about families and relationships

Level
upper-intermediate

Time
40–50 minutes

Preparation
one photocopy for each student

Extra notes
This activity should be treated with sensitivity with students who have suffered a family trauma. Dictionaries may be useful for this activity.

Warm-up

● Introduce the activity by asking students to write down which relative they think they most look like in their family. Ask a few students which relative they have written down, then find out the most common answer by a show of hands. If possible, bring in a photo of your own family and ask students to say who they think you look like.

Main activity

❶ Hand out a worksheet to each student. Ask students to look at the first set of questions. They are all connected to the family. Explain that they have to work in pairs to complete the sentences, using the words in the box. You may want to give definitions or hand out dictionaries.

❷ Give students a few minutes, then go through the answers together.

Answers
1 look   2 take   3 run   4 extended   5 generation   6 head   7 black   8 blood

❸ Next they ask each other the questions and discuss their answers together.

❹ Ask students some follow-up questions such as *Can you take after someone who isn't a member of your family? Are parents part of an extended family? Is there a generation gap between teachers and students?*

❺ Students work individually to draw their family tree, going back to their grandparents. Set a time limit of five minutes for this.

❻ Now reorganise students into groups of three or four. Ask them to present their family tree to their group, including interesting facts about their relatives. They should use the new vocabulary. Encourage the rest of the group to ask follow-up questions.

❼ Finish the activity by asking them to discuss the last set of questions in their groups. Then invite the whole class to share their ideas.

Follow-up

○ Ask students to write an essay with the title *Technology has made the generation gap bigger*. They should give plenty of reasons for their opinions and include lots of examples.

○ Students write an entertaining piece of fiction using as much of the key vocabulary as possible, e.g. *Tom was the black sheep of the family. He looked like his grandfather, with his large nose and dark eyes. He took after his mother because he was always laughing and joking, but he was very lazy.*

○ Ask students to bring in photos of their families to illustrate who they look like / take after. They can use them to illustrate a larger version of their family tree.

1   Work with a partner. Complete the sentences with the words in the box.

| extended | head | black | blood | run | look | generation | take |

1   Who do you _____ like the most?
2   Who do you _____ after?
3   What talents or abilities _____ in your family?
4   How much time do you spend with your _____ family?
5   Is there a _____ gap in your family?
6   Who do you think is the _____ of your family? Why?
7   Is there a _____ sheep in your family?
8   Do you think _____ is thicker than water? Why? / Why not?

2   Discuss the questions above with your partner.

3   Draw your family tree here. Start with your grandparents at the top and finish with you, your brothers, sisters and cousins at the bottom.

4   Present your family tree to your group. Include some interesting facts.

My grandfather's name was Victor. I never met him but my mother says I take after him ...

5   Discuss these questions in your group.
1   What can you learn from previous generations of your family?
2   Do you think intelligence runs in families or comes mostly from education?
3   Are people in your country today spending more or less time together as a family?
4   If you bring up children, how different will it be from how your parents brought you up?

Their day, your day, my day

Language focus
time; present simple questions

Key vocabulary
daily activities

Skills focus
speaking: exchanging information about routines

Level
elementary

Time
30 minutes

Preparation
one photocopy for each pair, cut into A and B parts

Warm-up

❶ Brainstorm daily routines with the students and write a list of activities on the board such as *get up, have lunch* and *go to bed.* Then practise saying times, e.g. *at eight o'clock, at half past twelve, at ten thirty, at five fifty-five.*

❷ Elicit a question for each of the activities on the board, e.g. *What time do you get up? When do you have lunch?* Invite a student to the front. Using the prompts on the board ask the others to question the student about his/her routine. Make sure the student doesn't forget to use the preposition *at* in the answers. Write the times he/she does things on the board next to the activities.

❸ Students now use the information on the board to practise asking and answering third-person questions, e.g. *What time does he/she get up?* You can make this into a memory game by gradually erasing some of the times or routines from the board. Encourage students to answer in full sentences so that they are practising the third person singular.

Main activity

❶ Put students in pairs. Hand out an A and a B worksheet to each pair. Explain that the two cards have different information. Students must not look at their partner's worksheet.

❷ Before they start, ask them to fill in the column headed *You* with the time they themselves do the activities.

❸ Explain that they have to take it in turns to ask and answer questions about Mark, Chloe, Jack and Lauren. They must use the information given to fill in the blank clocks.

❹ They should now question their partner about his/her routine to complete the final column.

❺ When they have finished they should compare their worksheets to see if they both have the correct solutions.

Follow-up

○ Ask students to write several sentences comparing their daily routine with their partner's, e.g. *I get up at seven o'clock but* (name) *gets up at half past six.*

○ Students write some more sentences comparing their usual daily routine with their weekend routine, e.g. *On Monday I get up at seven o'clock but on Saturday I get up at ten o'clock.*

○ In pairs, students plan an ideal routine for themselves on a school day. They can include different activites to those included on the worksheet, e.g. *We get up at nine o'clock. We go to school ten o'clock. We have a break at eleven o'clock. We do sports at eleven thirty.*

A

	Mark	Chloe	Jack	Lauren	You	Your partner
get up	6:30	(clock)	7:40	(clock)	(clock)	(clock)
go to school	(clock)	(clock)	7:55	8:15	(clock)	(clock)
have lunch	(clock)	1:30	12:45	(clock)	(clock)	(clock)
get home	4:10	(clock)	(clock)	5:00	(clock)	(clock)
have dinner	(clock)	6:00	(clock)	6:30	(clock)	(clock)
do homework	6:45	7:15	(clock)	(clock)	(clock)	(clock)
go to bed	(clock)	10:30	10:20	(clock)	(clock)	(clock)

✂ -

B

	Mark	Chloe	Jack	Lauren	You	Your partner
get up	(clock)	7:15	(clock)	7:00	(clock)	(clock)
go to school	7:25	8:00	(clock)	(clock)	(clock)	(clock)
have lunch	12:00	(clock)	(clock)	2:00	(clock)	(clock)
get home	(clock)	4:55	4:45	(clock)	(clock)	(clock)
have dinner	5:30	(clock)	7:00	(clock)	(clock)	(clock)
do homework	(clock)	(clock)	8:15	7:50	(clock)	(clock)
go to bed	10:15	(clock)	(clock)	10:00	(clock)	(clock)

Your week

Language focus
present simple, present continuous; expressions of frequency

Key vocabulary
habits; *at least, cinema, do exercise, hairdryer, news, relative*

Skills focus
speaking: asking about daily routines and future plans

Level
intermediate

Time
25 minutes

Preparation
one photocopy for each student

Warm-up

❶ Revise present simple and present continuous questions by writing sample answers on the board and using them to elicit questions. For example, *Twice a week* might be the answer to *How often do you watch a DVD?*; *Yes, I am, I've got a test tomorrow* might be the answer to *Are you studying this evening?*

❷ Invite students to give you more answers and make a list of them on the board. Only use those answers that practise the target grammar. Then elicit the questions for them.

Main activity

❶ Hand out a worksheet to each student. Explain to students that they will need to go round the class asking questions to fill in their worksheet. Their aim is to find a name to write on every line.

❷ Look at the first three or four items with the class and elicit the questions they will need to ask to find out the information, e.g. *How often do you travel by bus? What do you usually have for breakfast?* They may need to ask more than one question to obtain the information they need, e.g. *Do you play basketball?* followed by *How often do you play?* to find someone who plays basketball every week.

❸ Students circulate with their worksheets. Set a time limit of 15 minutes to find a person for each item. Point out that they can only use each name a maximum of three times. A small class may have to use each name more frequently. Make sure they ask full questions and do not show their worksheets to anyone else.

❹ Students sit down again and compare their results in pairs.

❺ With the whole class, choose individual students and ask them whether or not they found someone for all the items. Ask the class which were the hardest ones to find and talk about why.

❻ Find out if any of them knows who gets up the earliest, who goes to bed the latest or who is cooking this evening.

Follow-up

○ Ask students to work in groups and compare their weekday daily routines with their routines at the weekend. They can prepare ten questions about weekend habits and use them to construct a survey. After interviewing other students, they should write up their findings in a report.

○ Tell students that next weekend is going to be their perfect weekend. They can do whatever they want. Students prepare a description (oral or written) of their perfect weekend. They should present it as a schedule and use the present continuous, e.g. *On Saturday, I'm getting up at ten o'clock. I'm having breakfast at the Ritz with my friends.* Invite students to present their weekend to the class or put their schedule up on the classroom wall.

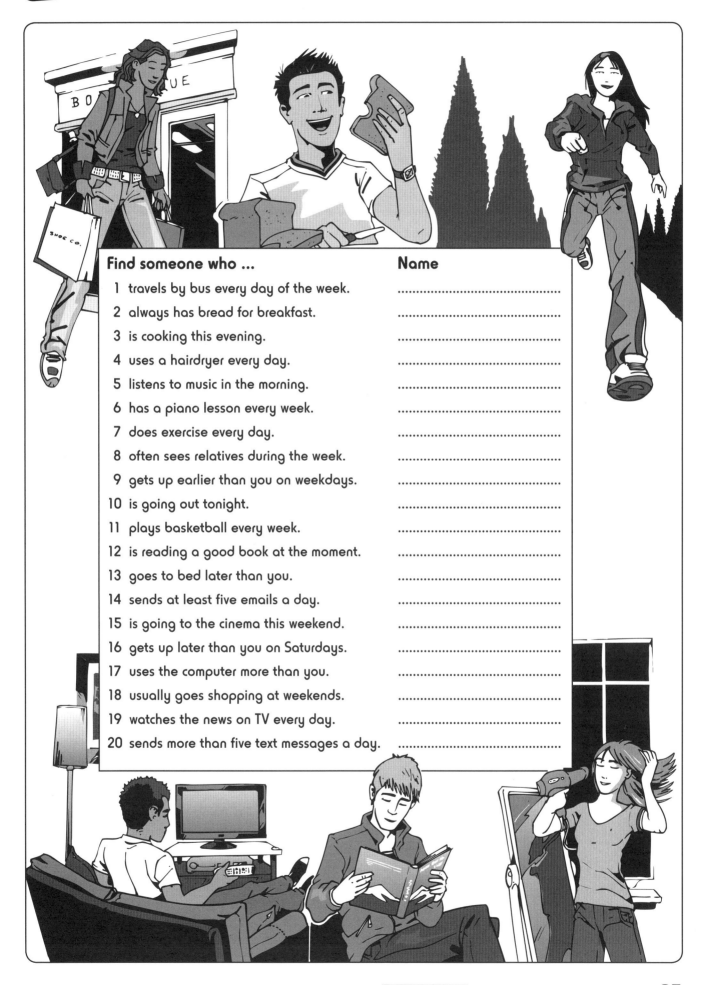

Find someone who ...   **Name**

1 travels by bus every day of the week.   ....

2 always has bread for breakfast.   ....

3 is cooking this evening.   ....

4 uses a hairdryer every day.   ....

5 listens to music in the morning.   ....

6 has a piano lesson every week.   ....

7 does exercise every day.   ....

8 often sees relatives during the week.   ....

9 gets up earlier than you on weekdays.   ....

10 is going out tonight.   ....

11 plays basketball every week.   ....

12 is reading a good book at the moment.   ....

13 goes to bed later than you.   ....

14 sends at least five emails a day.   ....

15 is going to the cinema this weekend.   ....

16 gets up later than you on Saturdays.   ....

17 uses the computer more than you.   ....

18 usually goes shopping at weekends.   ....

19 watches the news on TV every day.   ....

20 sends more than five text messages a day. ....

Board of life

Language focus
questions with *how often*; expressions of frequency

Key vocabulary
chat room, counter, download, have a lie-in, instead of, snack, toss a coin

Skills focus
speaking: talking about lifestyles; follow-up questions

Level
upper-intermediate

Time
40 minutes

Preparation
one photocopy for each group of 3 or 4 students; a coin for each group and a counter for each student; a photocopy of the Rules for each group (optional)

Extra notes
This activity is useful practice for a speaking exam.

Warm-up

❶ Write the words *sports* and *TV* on the board. Invite a student to the front of the class. Using the two prompts, elicit *How often* questions about his/her lifestyle, e.g. *How often do you do sports? How often do you watch TV?*

❷ Encourage students to ask follow-up questions such as *Where do you play (tennis)? Why do you like (tennis)? Do you have a TV in your bedroom? What kind of programmes do you like? Who's your favourite actor?*

❸ Invite a second student to the front and repeat the activity with the prompts *music* and *shopping*. Again make sure students ask follow-up questions such as *Have you got a favourite band? Who's your favourite singer? When do you listen to music? Where do you go shopping? What do you like shopping for best?*

Main activity

❶ Divide the class into groups of three or four and choose a scorer for each group. Hand out a board, four counters and a coin to each group. Make sure they know which side of the coin is 'heads' and which is 'tails'. The scorer needs paper and a pen.

❷ Explain the rules for this activity (see the Rules box below).

❸ While the game is being played, help with vocabulary and resolve any disputes about the questions being asked.

Follow-up

○ Students work in groups to prepare a lifestyle survey with ten or more new questions. They complete it by asking other class members, or students in a different class. They can follow this up with a written report on their findings, in the style of a newspaper report.

○ Students write an essay comparing the lifestyles of two different people of their choice (perhaps *parent/student; teacher / famous footballer*). They can expand this with opinions on who has the preferable lifestyle.

Rules for Board of life

1 Each player places their counter on square A, B, C or D. There must only be one counter on a square.

2 Take it in turns to toss the coin. If it is 'heads' move forward one square. If it is 'tails' move forward two squares.

3 When a player lands on a square, he/she makes a sentence about his/her lifestyle using the present simple and an expression of frequency, e.g. *I usually see my relatives once a month.*

4 The other players can ask one follow-up question each, e.g. *Which relative do you see most often?* The scorer gives a point for each correct and appropriate follow-up question. He/she writes down the score. The first player also gets a point for each follow-up question answered correctly.

5 When it is the scorer's turn, another player should become the scorer until he/she has finished.

6 The game ends when one player reaches their home square. The winner is the player with the most points.

3.3 Board of life

How often do you ...?

A ➡

take photographs

walk instead of travelling by car

cook

go on holiday

B ⬇

do exercise

argue with people

use an internet chat room

go to concerts

cycle

see your relatives

feel lonely

tidy your room

watch a film

download music

play computer games

spend too much money

eat fruit and vegetables

have a lie-in

go shopping

check your emails

wish your life was different

help with housework

D ⬆

think about your future

eat snacks between meals

meet your friends

read a book

C ⬅

When?

Why?

What?

Where?

Who?

What's different?

Language focus
there is/are; prepositions of place

Key vocabulary
furniture and household objects

Skills focus
speaking: describing the location of objects

Level
elementary

Time
25 minutes

Preparation
one photocopy for each pair, cut into A and B parts

Warm-up

❶ Write these letters on the board: *B, C, D, L, M, S, T, W.* Put students in pairs. Ask them to think of words beginning with these letters for things you can see inside a house or flat. Set a time limit of three or four minutes. Find out which pair has the most words.

❷ Ask the pair with the most words to write their list on the board. Invite others to add to it. Make sure these words are included: *bed, chair, computer, desk, DVD player, lamp, mirror, mouse, screen, shelf, sofa, speakers, table, television, wall, wardrobe, window.* You could draw sketches on the board to elicit any of these words that students have not mentioned.

Main activity

❶ Hand out an A and a B worksheet to each pair. Students must not look at their partner's worksheet.

❷ Explain to students that their pictures are very similar but not the same. They need to describe their rooms in detail to their partner. They should try to discover eight differences between their pictures and make a note of them on their worksheets.

❸ Set a time limit of ten minutes for the activity. Students then compare their pictures to make sure they have the correct information.

❹ With the whole class, elicit sentences describing the differences between the pictures. For example: *In my picture there's a lamp next to the cupboard, but in (name)'s picture the lamp is behind the sofa.*

Follow-up

○ Ask students to study their pictures and write a short description of the person who lives in the flat.

○ Practise requests. Give pairs the following notes:

Student A
In B's flat you want: *to wash your hair*; *to use the computer*; *to have a sandwich*
In your flat you have: *orange juice in fridge; DVD player not working; no washing machine*

Student B
In A's flat you want: *to have a drink*; *to watch a DVD*; *to wash your clothes*
In your flat you have: *shower in bathroom; computer on desk in bedroom; no bread*

Student A makes three requests and B responds, e.g.
A: *Can I wash my hair?*
B: *Yes, of course. There's a shower in the bathroom.*
A: *Can I have a sandwich?*
B: *No, sorry. I haven't got any bread.*

Then students swap roles. You could encourage them to add one or two more requests of their own.

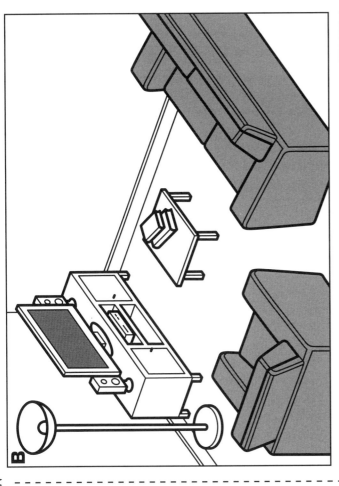

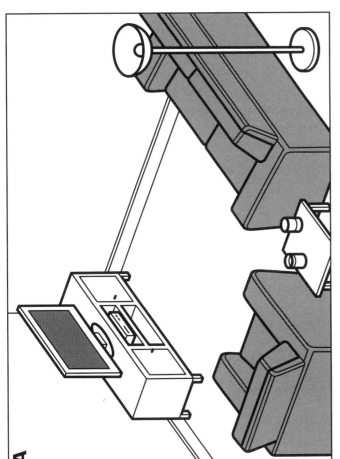

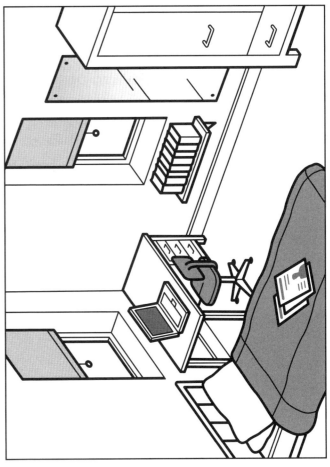

My home

Language focus
present simple; *would*; second conditional; comparative and superlative adjectives

Key vocabulary
rooms and household objects; places in a neighbourhood; *electrical appliance, ideal, miss, neighbour(hood), relaxing*

Skills focus
speaking: talking at length about homes and neighbourhoods; follow-up questions

Level
intermediate

Time
30 minutes

Preparation
one photocopy for each group of 3 or 4 students, cut into separate cards

Extra notes
This activity is useful practice for a speaking exam.

Warm-up

❶ Divide the class into two teams. Choose a secretary for each team. Ask team A to brainstorm ten things you find in a home (e.g. *living room*). Ask team B to brainstorm ten things you find in a neighbourhood (e.g. *park*). The secretaries write the list for their own team. Set a time limit of three minutes.

❷ When each team has a list of ten words ready, give team B one minute to try and guess team A's words. They can make as many guesses as they like in that minute. After each guess, A's secretary says if it is correct or incorrect. Give them a point for each correct word.

❸ Now team A has a turn to try and guess team B's words. The team with the most points wins.

Main activity

❶ Divide the class into groups of three or four. Give each group a set of cards, placed face down on the table.

❷ Tell students that they are going to talk about their homes and neighbourhoods.

❸ To demonstrate, take a card and read out the question. Answer it about yourself and speak for about half a minute. Encourage students to ask you follow-up questions. Now ask one of the students the same question.

❹ Explain that they have to take it in turns to pick a card and ask the student sitting on their right the question. He/she should speak for about half a minute, then the others ask follow-up questions.

❺ End the activity by asking each student to tell the class something interesting they discovered about someone in their group.

Follow-up

○ Set up a project where students plan an ideal neighbourhood. Each group produces a poster to advertise their neighbourhood and then presents it to the class. Students vote on the poster they like best.

○ Ask students to write an essay entitled *What I like about where I live*.

Describe your living room.

Describe the street where you live.

What's the most important thing in your home? Why?

Do you like your neighbours? Why? / Why not?

How many electrical appliances are there in your home? What are they?

Do you think your neighbourhood is a nice place to live? Why? / Why not?

What would make your neighbourhood a better place to live?

What do you miss about your home when you're not there?

Describe your ideal home.

What would make your home a better place?

Do you think it's better to live in a city or in the country? Why?

What's the best thing about your neighbourhood?

Where do you spend most time in your home? Why?

Which is the most relaxing room in your home?

What is there to do in your free time in your neighbourhood?

Where do you go most often in your neighbourhood?

If you could choose any object to have in your home, what would it be?

Where would you like to live in the future?

Describe your bedroom.

Which is your favourite room in your home and why?

My area

Language focus
language of opinions;
connectors

Key vocabulary
opinion phrases;
*countryside, cultural,
keep fit, local, public
transport, retired*

Skills focus
speaking: expressing
opinions about
neighbourhoods;
justifying decisions

Level
upper-intermediate

Time
45 minutes

Preparation
one photocopy for each
student

Warm-up

1 Explain the word *neighbourhood*. Introduce the theme of *my area* by prompting students to ask you questions about the neighbourhood you live in. You may want to write a few prompts on the board such as *swimming pool, cinema, shops* and *café*.
You might find it useful to put some question openers on the board:
Is/Are there …?
Have you got ?
Do you live near ?
What's / What are the … like?
Is the neighbourhood (adjective)?

2 Invite a student to the front. Ask the others to ask similar questions about his/her neighbourhood.

Main activity

1 Hand out a worksheet to each student. Ask them to imagine they are moving to a new area. Give them five minutes working alone to look at the features and decide which they think are the most important. Tell them to write in pencil so they can make changes to this ranking after the following discussion. They have to put the numbers in the boxes. Set a time limit of five minutes.

2 When students have finished, divide them into pairs. Tell them to compare their lists using the language of opinions. You may want to put some useful phrases on the board, e.g. *I don't agree because … On the other hand … Yes, you're right but …* Each pair has to negotiate a new list of the eight most important things.

3 Now put pairs together to make groups of four. Ask the two sets of pairs to compare their lists and justify their choices.

4 Students stay in groups of four and talk about what they would like in their own area that isn't there at present. They should give reasons for their choices.

5 Ask students to read the descriptions of Emily and James, Danielle and Bob and Margaret. In their groups, students have to decide on four things (from the original list) that would be most important for these people. They will need to make three different lists. Set a time limit of seven minutes.

6 Groups give feedback to the whole class on their choices and the reasons behind their decisions. Once again, encourage them to use the language of agreeing and disagreeing.

7 Finally, ask students to decide which of these people would most enjoy living in their own area and why. Exchange ideas as a whole class.

Follow-up

○ In groups, students design and perform a TV advert to attract people to move to the area where they live. They could even film each other and then vote on the best advert.

○ In groups, students prepare a short computer presentation entitled *My ideal area*. This could include visuals of the most important features.

1   Look at the list below. Which do you think are most important when you choose
    a town to live in? Put 1 for the most important and 16 for the least important.

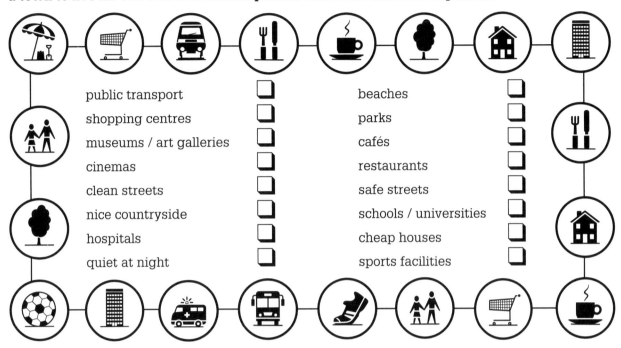

public transport ☐
shopping centres ☐
museums / art galleries ☐
cinemas ☐
clean streets ☐
nice countryside ☐
hospitals ☐
quiet at night ☐

beaches ☐
parks ☐
cafés ☐
restaurants ☐
safe streets ☐
schools / universities ☐
cheap houses ☐
sports facilities ☐

2   Compare your answers with a partner. Together, decide the eight most important things. Then
    compare your decisions with another pair.

3   Which things would you most like to have in your area? Why? Discuss this with your group.

4   Look at the descriptions of some people below. With a partner, choose four things from the
    list that would be most important for each of them.

Emily and **James** have been
married for eight years and
have two children, aged five and
three. They both like keeping fit
in their spare time.

Danielle has just left university
and has got a job in the local
bank. She lives alone and would
like to meet new people and
make friends. She can't drive.

Bob and **Margaret** have
been married for forty years and
have just retired. They enjoy
walking and cultural activities,
but don't really like noisy places.

5   Which person/people would most enjoy living in your area? Why?

In town

Language focus
prepositions; present simple

Key vocabulary
shops and buildings in town; directions; prepositions

Skills focus
reading and speaking: describing location; giving directions

Level
elementary

Time
25 minutes

Preparation
one photocopy for each pair, cut into A and B parts

Extra notes
The teacher's version of the map (key) is on page 118. You may want to photocopy this.

Warm-up

❶ Revise words for places in town. Give prompts to elicit the words, e.g. *You can buy bread at the … (baker's), You can buy CDs at the … (music shop), You can see paintings at the … (art gallery), You can watch films at the … (cinema), You can go across a river on a … (bridge), You can catch a train at the … (station)*, etc.

❷ Choose three students to come to the front of the class. Move them into different positions to elicit sentences with *near, next to, in front of, opposite, between, in the corner, in the middle, on the left/right.*

Main activity

❶ Put students in pairs and hand out an A and a B worksheet to each pair. Students must not look at their partner's worksheet.

❷ Explain that they have the same map with different information. They need to share their information to identify the places that are without labels on their map. These places are listed at the bottom of their worksheet.

❸ Read out the following sentences as an example: *They make toys in this building. It's at the end of North Road and it's near the station.* Elicit *(toy) factory* and tell students to write this label on the correct building on their map. Check that they have written it in the right place by referring to the teacher's map on page 118. It's important for the activity that they label this correctly.

❹ Students take it in turns to read out the sentences on their worksheets. After each sentence they look at their maps and help each other to locate and label the relevant buildings. They will often find that there are two possibilities to choose between, but their partner can give them the necessary information to get the right answer. Make sure that they exchange information orally, without showing their map to their partner.

❺ Students each check the list of places at the bottom of their worksheet. If any of these are still missing on their map, they ask their partner questions to find out where they are, for example:
A: *Where's the phone shop?*
B: *It's in North Road, next to the sports shop. It's opposite the art gallery.*

❻ At the end, students compare their maps. If there are any differences, they should reread the sentences to determine the correct answers.

Follow-up

⭕ Ask questions about the map. Students listen and write the answers. Examples:
Come out of the music shop. What's on your left? (the newsagent's)
Come out of the police station, turn left and go across Queens Road. What's the building on your right? (the hotel)
Stand in the middle of the main square and look at the school. What's behind you on the opposite corner? (the post office)
Come out of the station, walk through the car park and cross the road. Where are you? (outside / in front of the library)

⭕ Ask students to use the map and write directions from one place to another, e.g. from the cinema to the sports shop. They should name the starting point but not the destination. In pairs, they read each other's directions and work out the destination.

A

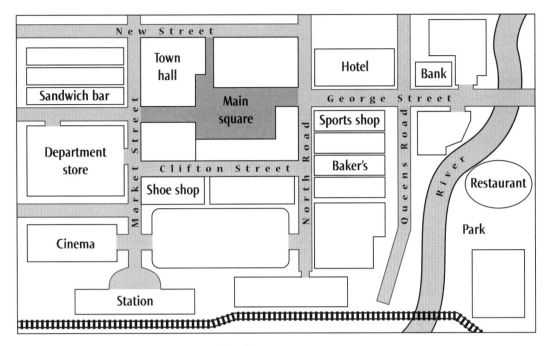

1 The museum is in George Street, next to the river.
2 You can post a letter in this building. It's in Clifton Street, next to the art gallery.
3 When you come out of the cinema, the car park is in front of you.
4 The clothes shop is opposite the art gallery. It isn't in the main square.

You should be able to label these places on your map: art gallery, car park, clothes shop, internet café, library, museum, music shop, newsagent's, phone shop, police station, post office, school, sports centre.

B

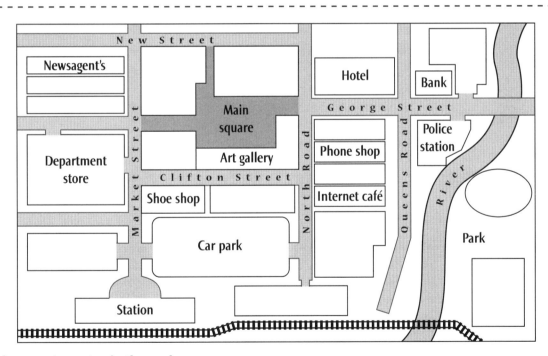

1 There's a sports centre in the park.
2 The school is in the main square, near the town hall.
3 You can buy CDs in this shop. It's between the newsagent's and the sandwich bar.
4 The library is in North Road. It isn't next to a shop.

You should be able to label these places on your map: baker's, cinema, clothes shop, library, museum, music shop, post office, restaurant, sandwich bar, school, sports centre, sports shop, town hall.

The way to go

Language focus
mixed tenses

Key vocabulary
forms of transport;
verbs connected with
travelling

Skills focus
writing and speaking:
asking questions about
transport and travel

Level
intermediate

Time
40 minutes

Preparation
one photocopy for
2 students, cut into A
and B parts; mix up the
2 sets of photocopies so
you can distribute them
randomly

Warm-up

❶ Put students in pairs. Give them two minutes to think of all the words they can for forms of transport. Ask the pair with the most words to read out their list and invite others to add to it. Write the words on the board.

❷ Then write these verbs on the board: *drive, catch, ride, fly, sail*. Ask students to match them with the transport words already on the board, e.g. *drive a car/ bus/lorry; catch a bus/train/ferry; ride a horse/bike/motorbike; fly (in) a plane/helicopter; sail (on) a boat/ship.*

Main activity

❶ Hand out the worksheets. Give half of the students the A version and the other half the B version.

❷ Explain to students that they need to go round the class asking questions to fill in their worksheet. Their aim is to find a name to write in every box in the second column. In the third column they should make a note of any extra information they get from the people they have named.

❸ Make it clear that there are two different worksheets, so students will not all have the same questions to ask.

❹ Take the first items in the two worksheets as examples and elicit questions: *Do you (always) get to school by bus? / How do you get to school? Do you want to learn to drive?*
Choose students to answer these questions. Ask a few follow-up questions to elicit extra information, e.g. *Where do you catch the bus? How long does the trip take?*

❺ Ask students to write down the questions they will ask. Monitor to check tenses.

❻ Students mingle, asking and answering. Because there are two worksheets, they will sometimes be answering on matters they have thought about while at other times they will have to respond to questions they won't be expecting. Set a time limit of 15 minutes for the activity.

❼ At the end, call out the name of each student in turn. Using their worksheets, other students give one or two pieces of information about each person, e.g. *She can ski. She enjoys cycling and she's got a really good mountain bike.*

Follow-up

○ Ask students to write four sentences about their transport habits and experiences, three true and one false. In pairs, they read each other's sentences, pick the one they think is false and explain why they think so. Their partner either confirms or corrects the answer.

○ Bring in copies of a map of the world. In groups, students plan a world trip using a variety of forms of transport. The groups then present their itinerary to the class. Encourage them to question and comment on each other's ideas.

5.2 The way to go

A

Find someone who ...	Name	Extra information
1 always gets to school by bus.		
2 has travelled by ferry.		
3 would like to drive a lorry.		
4 knows how to ski.		
5 isn't interested in cars.		
6 takes a long time to get home from school.		
7 can skateboard.		
8 went somewhere by car yesterday.		
9 enjoys cycling.		
10 has never flown in a plane.		
11 travelled abroad last year.		
12 is going to catch a train tomorrow.		
13 has got some inline skates.		
14 was travelling on public transport at 8.15 this morning.		

✂ -

B

Find someone who ...	Name	Extra information
1 wants to learn to drive.		
2 walked home from school yesterday.		
3 hasn't got a bike.		
4 has never travelled by coach.		
5 has been on a ship.		
6 sometimes goes running.		
7 is interested in sailing.		
8 would like to fly in a helicopter.		
9 is going to travel to another country soon.		
10 lives near a station.		
11 can't ride a horse.		
12 made a long train trip last year.		
13 doesn't like flying.		
14 was waiting at a bus stop between 4.00 and 5.00 pm yesterday.		

Around the world in 25 days

Language focus
language of suggestions;
future with *will* and
going to

Key vocabulary
language connected
with travel

Skills focus
speaking: making plans;
expressing opinions;
giving a presentation

Level
upper-intermediate

Time
50 minutes

Preparation
one photocopy for each
student

Extra notes
Atlases would be useful
for this activity, or access
to the Internet.

Warm-up

❶ Write the following places on the board: *Galapagos Islands, Grand Canyon, Great Barrier Reef, Kilimanjaro, Lake Titicaca, Mont Blanc, Niagara Falls, Pyramids, River Rhine, Taj Mahal, Uluru* and *Yangtze River.* Ask students to match each place to a continent.

❷ Ask them what they can tell you about the famous sites on the board. You can help them with questions such as *What did the Egyptians build for their dead kings? What's the highest mountain in Africa? What's the longest river in China?*

Main activity

❶ Divide students into groups of three or four. Hand out a worksheet to each student.

❷ Explain the situation and tell them to make their plans together. Make sure they understand all the rules about countries and continents. Explain that they can only travel in one direction throughout (from east to west or west to east).

❸ In their groups, they first decide the order they will visit the countries in and make a list on the worksheet. Remind them that they should use different means of transport. They will need to allow for travelling time in their plans.

❹ Next ask them to look at the blank plan and decide how long they will spend in each country. They need to fill this in at the top of the square for each day.

❺ Now ask them to plan what they will do each day. They should try to make the trip as exciting and interesting as possible, including natural and man-made wonders, famous cities, places of beauty, adventurous or relaxing activities. You may want to give them examples of useful openers, e.g.
I (don't) want to / I'd like to …
We should …
Let's … / How about … ? / Why don't we …?

❻ Explain that they will present the most exciting part of their trip to the class. Each member of the group must speak in the presentation. Allow them five to ten minutes to prepare their notes and decide who will say what. They should use *going to* and *will* for the presentation.

❼ Groups take it in turns to come to the front of the class and make their presentations. Encourage other groups to ask questions about the trips.

❽ The whole class votes for the best presentation. The winning group's plan will be the one used for the class trip.

Follow-up

◉ Ask students to write an entry from a travel blog describing one of the days of their trip.

◉ As an extension, students use the Internet to produce an advertising poster or brochure for their trip, including photos and interesting facts.

1 Your class has won a ticket to travel around the world. Your group has to suggest a plan.
You can travel to a maximum of eight different countries. You must visit at least three
different continents. Include travel by boat, by train and by air. You must always travel in the
same direction, from east to west or west to east. In your group, decide what places you will visit
and the order you will visit them in. List the countries below.

1 _____   5 _____

2 _____   6 _____

3 _____   7 _____

4 _____   8 _____

2 The whole trip is 25 days long. In your group, decide how long you will spend in each country.
Write the country at the top of each day. Then decide what you will do each day and make
notes in the squares.

Day 1	Day 2	Day 3	Day 4	Day 5
Day 6	Day 7	Day 8	Day 9	Day 10
Day 11	Day 12	Day 13	Day 14	Day 15
Day 16	Day 17	Day 18	Day 19	Day 20
Day 21	Day 22	Day 23	Day 24	Day 25

3 In your group, present the most exciting part of your trip to the class.

Our birthdays

Language focus
dates; *in* + month; *on* +
date; possessive *'s*

Key vocabulary
months; ordinal
numbers

Skills focus
speaking: asking for and
giving dates

Level
elementary

Time
25 minutes

Preparation
one photocopy for each
student

Warm-up

❶ If necessary, revise dates. Write today's date on the board and remind students how to say it: *the (ordinal) of (month)*. Write other dates on the board in figures (e.g. *25/7, 3/9, 22/12, 31/8*) and ask students to say them.

❷ Ask a student: *When's your birthday?* and elicit the answer *It's on (date)*. Invite the class to ask you the same question and give the answer. Then ask: *Who has a birthday in (June)?* and ask students to raise their hands. You may want to write the two questions on the board.

Main activity

❶ Hand out the calendar worksheets. Ask students to mark their own birthday by circling the date and labelling it with their name.

❷ Divide the class in half (groups A and B). Students circulate within their group, asking *When's your birthday?* They circle all the dates and label the names on their calendar. They will need to write small to fit in the names.

❸ Now put students in pairs, with one partner from group A and the other from group B. They take it in turns to ask: *Whose birthday is in (month)?* and fill in the information on their calendar. At the end, students should have a record of all the birthdays in the class.

❹ Ask the class questions to extract information from the calendar, for example:
Which month has the most birthdays?
Do any people have the same birthday?
Who has a birthday in the spring/winter (etc.)?
Does anyone have a birthday in the summer holidays?
Whose birthday is at the beginning/end of the month?
How many people were born in January/March (etc.)?
Whose birthday is the first in the year?
Who had a birthday recently?
Whose birthday is next?

❺ Invite students to describe other dates in the year that are important to them, for example: *My sister's birthday is on (date). The summer holidays start on (date). Justin Timberlake was born on 31st January.*

Follow-up

○ Keep a copy of the calendar yourself so that you can organise a small celebration when a student's birthday comes up.

○ Ask students to find out about a few famous people of their choice on the Internet. Ask them to make a poster with pictures of these people and their names, ages and birthdays underneath.

January						
1	2	3	4	5	6	7
8	9	10	11	12	13	14
15	16	17	18	19	20	21
22	23	24	25	26	27	28
29	30	31				

February						
1	2	3	4	5	6	7
8	9	10	11	12	13	14
15	16	17	18	19	20	21
22	23	24	25	26	27	28
29						

March						
1	2	3	4	5	6	7
8	9	10	11	12	13	14
15	16	17	18	19	20	21
22	23	24	25	26	27	28
29	30	31				

April						
1	2	3	4	5	6	7
8	9	10	11	12	13	14
15	16	17	18	19	20	21
22	23	24	25	26	27	28
29	30					

May						
1	2	3	4	5	6	7
8	9	10	11	12	13	14
15	16	17	18	19	20	21
22	23	24	25	26	27	28
29	30	31				

June						
1	2	3	4	5	6	7
8	9	10	11	12	13	14
15	16	17	18	19	20	21
22	23	24	25	26	27	28
29	30					

July						
1	2	3	4	5	6	7
8	9	10	11	12	13	14
15	16	17	18	19	20	21
22	23	24	25	26	27	28
29	30	31				

August						
1	2	3	4	5	6	7
8	9	10	11	12	13	14
15	16	17	18	19	20	21
22	23	24	25	26	27	28
29	30	31				

September						
1	2	3	4	5	6	7
8	9	10	11	12	13	14
15	16	17	18	19	20	21
22	23	24	25	26	27	28
29	30					

October						
1	2	3	4	5	6	7
8	9	10	11	12	13	14
15	16	17	18	19	20	21
22	23	24	25	26	27	28
29	30	31				

November						
1	2	3	4	5	6	7
8	9	10	11	12	13	14
15	16	17	18	19	20	21
22	23	24	25	26	27	28
29	30					

December						
1	2	3	4	5	6	7
8	9	10	11	12	13	14
15	16	17	18	19	20	21
22	23	24	25	26	27	28
29	30	31				

Festivals quiz

Language focus
Wh- questions; dates

Key vocabulary
festivals and
celebrations; countries
and nationalities

Skills focus
reading and speaking:
discussing and
answering quiz
questions

Level
intermediate

Time
30 minutes

Preparation
one photocopy for each
group of 3 or 4 students

Extra notes
To change the focus
from reading to
listening, you can read
out the quiz questions
instead of handing out
the worksheet. Groups
write their answers on a
sheet of paper.

Warm-up

❶ Get students thinking about the topic by asking them to name some of the most important festivals in their own country.

❷ Then brainstorm names of festivals and special days in other parts of the world. Don't go into details here, as this could take away some of the challenge of the quiz.

Main activity

❶ Organise the class in groups of three or four. Ask them to choose a group leader who will record their answers and make a decision if there is any disagreement.

❷ Hand out a quiz worksheet to each group. Set a time limit of 15 minutes for groups to discuss and answer the questions. If they don't know some of the answers, encourage them to guess. You may want to explain that *blossom* means the flowers that appear on trees in the spring.

❸ When they are ready, they exchange worksheets with another group to mark the answers. Go through the answers with the class and follow up with further questions and/or brief discussion. Groups score one point for each correct answer.

❹ You could give out small prizes to the group that scores the most points.

Answers

1 24th December (or 5th/6th January for Orthodox Christians)   2 February
3 autumn/fall   4 1st January   5 one month   6 31st October

7 USA   8 France   9 Japan (other Asian cherry blossom festivals exist, e.g. in South Korea and parts of China)   10 the Chinese   11 the Irish
12 Germany   13 Venice   14 Rio de Janeiro   15 Mexico
16 Spain (Pamplona)

17 New Year / New Year's Eve   18 Halloween   19 Ramadan   20 Carnival, Halloween (other answers are also possible)   21 Easter

22 roses   23 (chocolate) eggs   24 turkey   25 thirteen   26 the day after Christmas / 26th December   27 red   28 Because it is a festival of light.
29 women (it is International Women's Day)   30 Because on this day people remember the soldiers who died in wars.

Follow-up

○ Ask groups to write four or five new quiz questions for the rest of the class on festivals in their own country or elsewhere in the world. They could do some research on the Internet to obtain or check information.

○ Invite groups to invent a special day to be celebrated at their school. They should think about what the celebration is about, when the event takes place and what happens on that day. Groups then share their ideas with the class. Examples of celebrations might include *a school carnival, a football or music festival, a celebration for the beginning of summer* or for *someone's birthday*.

6.2 Festivals quiz

Name the time

1 What date is Christmas Eve? _____
2 In which month is Valentine's Day? _____
3 In which season do Americans celebrate Thanksgiving? _____
4 What date is officially New Year's Day in Europe? _____
5 How long does Ramadan last? _____
6 What date is Halloween? _____

Name the place or people

7 Which country has Independence Day on 4th July? _____
8 Which country has its national day on 14th July? _____
9 Which Asian country has a famous festival of cherry blossom? _____
10 Who has a 15-day celebration for New Year in January or February? _____
11 Who celebrates St Patrick's Day? _____
12 Which country started the tradition of Christmas trees? _____
13 Which Italian city is famous for its carnival masks and costumes? _____
14 Which city in South America has the biggest carnival in the world? _____
15 Which Latin American country has a very famous Day of the Dead in November? _____
16 Where do people run through the streets with bulls in July? _____

Name the festival

17 Which celebration is associated with fireworks at midnight? _____
18 Which festival is associated with witches, ghosts and pumpkins? _____
19 Name a festival when people don't eat during the day. _____
20 Name two festivals when people dress in costumes. _____
21 Which festival does Good Friday belong to? _____

Extra questions

22 What flowers are associated with Valentine's Day? _____
23 What do children usually get at Easter? _____
24 What bird is traditionally cooked at Thanksgiving? _____
25 How old are most Jewish boys when they have their Bar Mitzvah? _____
26 What is Boxing Day? _____
27 What is the luckiest colour for Chinese celebrations? _____
28 Why are there so many lamps, candles and fireworks at the Hindu festival of Diwali? _____
29 Who has a special day on 8th March? _____
30 Why is there a day in November called Remembrance Day in some countries? _____

A new festival

Language focus
past, present and future tenses

Key vocabulary
festivals and celebrations

Skills focus
writing and speaking: organising information; note taking; giving a presentation

Level
upper-intermediate

Time
50–60 minutes

Preparation
one photocopy for each group of 3 or 4 students, cut into separate cards and mixed in a random order

Extra notes
The activity cards can be used to present a real festival rather than an invented one. The activity may also be spread over two lessons, depending on the size of the class and the amount of preparation time you want to give to it (see main activity 4).

Warm-up

❶ Ask students to give examples of traditional celebrations and festivals in their country. Make sure they include local events as well as big national ones. Focus on one of the festivals and invite students to say what they know about its origins and traditions.

❷ Then ask students to say which festival might seem most unusual to a foreign visitor to the country. If possible, briefly describe one or two particularly unusual festivals in other parts of the world, e.g. the Cooper's Hill Cheese Rolling races in Gloucestershire, England; La Tomatina (tomato fight) in Buñol, Spain; the Todd River boat races on a dry river bed in Alice Springs, Australia.

Main activity

❶ Organise the class in groups of three or four students. Explain that they are going to invent a new and unusual festival in their country and present it to the class. Set a time limit of five minutes to come up with some general ideas.

❷ Hand out a set of cards to each group. Ask them to choose at least 15 of the cards and use them to fill out the details of their festival. They can write notes on the cards. Encourage them to be inventive and to have fun with their ideas.

❸ Ask groups to put the cards in a logical sequence to organise their presentation and to decide who will say what.

❹ Groups practise their presentation. You may want to give them extra time to collect pictures, costumes, masks, posters, etc. to make the presentation more entertaining. Alternatively, they could prepare a computer presentation.

❺ In turn, groups present their festival to the class. Encourage the others to ask questions after each presentation.

❻ At the end, take a class vote on the best festival.

Follow-up

○ Ask students to imagine that their festival has just taken place. Ask them to write an internet blog describing their experience of the day.

○ Ask students to write a paragraph on their festival (or on a real festival in their country) for a tourist brochure or website.

name of festival	place(s)	date and duration
season and weather	number of people who take part	visitors and tourists
origins – when? why?	how it used to be	changes since it first began
preparations	what happens first	what happens later
highlight(s) of the event	costumes	decorations
music	special food	how and when the event ends
problems in the past	success or failure last year	plans for the future

Eating habits

Language focus
present and past simple questions; expressions of frequency

Key vocabulary
food and drink; *cereal, chips, meal, vegetarian*

Skills focus
speaking: asking for and giving information about eating habits

Level
elementary

Time
30 minutes

Preparation
one photocopy for each student

Warm-up

❶ Write the following words as a list on the board: *cola, tomatoes, thirsty, lunch, sandwich, meat.* Then put up the following prompts: *How often …? Do you …? Are you …? Can you …? Did you …?*

❷ Use the words with the prompts to elicit questions similar to those students will ask during the activity, e.g. *How often do you drink cola? Do you like tomatoes? Are you thirsty? Can you make a sandwich? Did you have meat yesterday?*

Main activity

❶ Hand out a worksheet to each student and revise or introduce the food words that appear.

❷ Ask students to think of a question that will give them the information they need for the first item, e.g. *How often do you eat chocolate?* or *Do you eat chocolate every day?*

❸ Elicit questions for the other items, correcting pronunciation as you go along. You may wish to keep the warm-up prompts on the board and add to them.

❹ Explain that students have to move around the class with their worksheets, asking questions, in order to find a person's name for each item. They can only use each person's name a maximum of two or three times. Set a time limit of 20 minutes.

❺ When they are ready, ask students to sit down in pairs. Tell them to compare their answers to see how often they come up with the same name.

❻ Finally, ask them to report back to the whole class.

Follow-up

○ Ask students to write a paragraph about the food they eat during a normal day, or on a special occasion.

○ In pairs, students make a questionnaire to find out the most popular food and drink in the class, what time people eat and other questions of their choice related to food. After conducting this research they can present their findings in a report with graphs or tables.

○ Tell students to make an ideal menu of the food they like best. Alternatively, they could make a nightmare menu of the dishes they hate! Display these around the classroom.

Find someone who ...	Name
1 ... eats chocolate every day.	
2 ... doesn't like lemonade.	
3 ... ate fish yesterday.	
4 ... had cereal for breakfast this morning.	
5 ... never drinks tea.	
6 ... eats fruit every day.	
7 ... drank coffee last night.	
8 ... can cook a meal.	
9 ... ate in a restaurant last week.	
10 ... feels hungry now.	
11 ... is a vegetarian.	
12 ... never eats bread.	
13 ... doesn't eat breakfast.	
14 ... watches TV while they eat.	
15 ... had a cake for his/her last birthday.	
16 ... likes pizza.	
17 ... ate chips last night.	
18 ... eats dinner at eight o'clock.	
19 ... goes shopping for food with his/her parents.	
20 ... can make a cup of coffee.	

Who's coming to dinner?

Language focus
going to for plans;
will for predictions;
prepositions of place

Key vocabulary
descriptions of food;
dinner party, guest, main course, seating plan, serve, starter

Skills focus
speaking: planning a function; expressing opinions; making predictions; giving a presentation

Level
intermediate

Time
45–60 minutes

Preparation
one photocopy for each pair

Extra notes
Students may have difficulties explaining food dishes in English; it may be useful to prepare a list of popular dishes for reference.
The final presentations could be done in a subsequent lesson; students could prepare a computer presentation.

Warm-up

❶ Ask students if they have ever been to a dinner party. Discuss whether they would prefer to have a dinner party at home or in a restaurant.

❷ Find out if they have ever been to a party when someone famous has been there. Ask them to imagine, if they could choose anyone, who they would like to meet at a party.

Main activity

❶ Divide the class into pairs. Hand out a worksheet to each pair. Explain that they are going to plan a special dinner party. They can invite eight guests. The guests must be famous but can be from the past or the present. They will be able to speak English, even if it's not their own language.

❷ Tell students to work with their partner to decide who to invite and then complete their guest list together. Encourage them to use the language of expressing opinions and agreeing and disagreeing. You may want to put some useful phrases on the board.

❸ Tell the pairs that they now have to plan their dinner menu together. They should describe the food in detail. They will probably need help with this, especially if they want to describe any national dishes.

❹ Next they decide on the seating plan, including themselves. They must arrange the guests in a way that will keep everyone happy and lead to interesting conversations.

❺ Now each pair prepares a presentation of their dinner party (the guests, the food and the seating plan). They will have to give reasons for their choices and explain why their dinner party will be a big success. Set a time limit of ten minutes for the preparation.

❻ Students present their plans. Depending on the size of your class, this can be done as a whole class or by putting students into groups. If you run out of time, the presentations can be given in a follow-up lesson.

Follow-up

◯ In pairs, students role play a conversation with one of the dinner guests they have invited. This could be the student talking to a guest, or two of the guests talking to each other.

◯ Ask students to decide on a small gift to give the dinner guests. All the dinner guests will receive the same gift, so it should be something that will appeal to all of them. If your students are all from the same place, you may like to encourage them to think of a gift that typifies their country or their town.

◯ In pairs, students design an invitation to their dinner party.

1 You are going to have a dinner party for yourself, your partner, and eight famous guests. The guests can be from the past or the present. Work with your partner and choose eight guests.

Guest list

1 ....   5 ....

2 ....   6 ....

3 ....   7 ....

4 ....   8 ....

2 Your meal will have a starter, a main course (including vegetables) and a dessert. Work with your partner and decide what food you will serve.

Menu

Starter: ....

Main course: ....

....

Dessert: ....

3 Where are the guests going to sit? Work with your partner and decide on the seating plan.

Name:	Name:	Name:	Name:

Name:	Table	Name:

Name:	Name:	Name:	Name:

4 Now present your dinner party plans to other students. Include the guest list, the menu and the seating plan. Give reasons for your choices and explain why your dinner party will be a big success.

Healthy eating

Language focus
present simple; *should*

Key vocabulary
food and nutrition;
*carbohydrate, column,
dairy, fat, pyramid,
typical*

Skills focus
writing and speaking:
categorising and making
lists; discussing eating
habits

Level
upper-intermediate

Time
45 minutes

Preparation
one photocopy for each
student

Extra notes
In the discussion part
of this activity you could
introduce the following
words: *high in …,
low in …, minerals,
protein, vitamins.*

Warm-up

❶ Introduce the topic of healthy eating by asking students if they eat fast food. Then ask them what the problems of unhealthy eating are.

❷ Discuss whether they or their parents choose what they eat. Which do they think is better?

Main activity

❶ Divide students into pairs. Hand out a worksheet to each student. Ask them to look at the list of food words together and place them in the right columns. Point out that there is not always a *correct* answer as the healthiness of some foods is a matter of opinion. Set a time limit of eight minutes.

❷ When they are ready, ask them to add at least five more words to each group.

❸ Find out if all the pairs have made the same decisions about the foods. They take it in turns to tell the class what other foods they added to the lists. Encourage students to justify their decisions. You may want to introduce the vocabulary of nutrition at this point.

❹ Look at the pyramid and explain that healthy eating involves eating more of the foods at the base of the pyramid, and less of the foods at the top. Ask students to look at their lists of healthy and unhealthy foods and decide where each food fits in the pyramid. Discuss the answers with the class.

❺ Students think about their typical diet and decide if it is healthy. They should refer to the healthy eating pyramid. They must identify five foods they should eat less of, and five foods they should eat more of. They discuss their choices with their partner. Encourage them to use phrases like *too much/many* and *not enough.*

❻ In pairs, students plan a healthy lunch menu for a school for five days. They will need to choose a main course, dessert and drink for each day. Explain that they should try to include plenty of different foods and make the menu appealing for teenagers.

❼ They present one day of their menu to the rest of the class (or to groups if this would take too long). The class makes comments on whether the choice of food is tasty, healthy, expensive or suitable for a vegetarian.

Follow-up

⭕ Set up a debate on the topic *Fast food is best*. Students should prepare by writing down some arguments *for* and some arguments *against* the statement.

⭕ Ask students to do some research on the Internet to find out which countries have the healthiest diet and which the least healthy. They may want to compare Japanese and American diets.

⭕ Students assess their national cuisine in terms of healthiness and suggest improvements.

1 Which of these foods do you think are healthy? Which are unhealthy if we eat or drink them often? Work with a partner and put them in the columns.

> apples   beefburgers   bread   butter   carrots   cheese
> chips   chocolate   cola   eggs   fish   fruit juice   garlic
> lemonade   milk   olive oil   oranges   pears   pizza
> rice   salt   sausages   spaghetti   tomatoes   water   yoghurt

HEALTHY	UNHEALTHY

How many other foods can you add to the columns?

2 Look at the healthy eating pyramid. What should you eat most/least?
Decide with a partner which category the foods in the table above belong to.

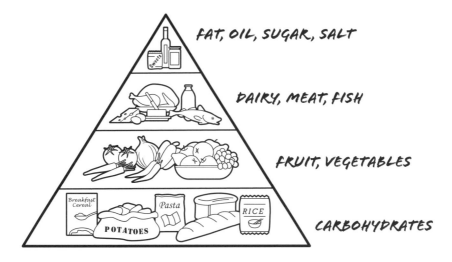

FAT, OIL, SUGAR, SALT

DAIRY, MEAT, FISH

FRUIT, VEGETABLES

CARBOHYDRATES

3 Think about what you eat in a typical week.
Complete the lists below, then compare your answers with a partner.

FIVE FOODS I SHOULD EAT MORE OFTEN	FIVE FOODS I SHOULD EAT LESS OFTEN
....	....
....	....
....	....
....	....
....	....

What can you see?

Language focus
present continuous questions and statements; *have got*

Key vocabulary
clothes; verbs for everyday actions; *baseball cap, glasses, jeans, play the guitar, poster, sell, shorts, sunglasses, wear*

Skills focus
speaking: describing actions and clothing

Level
elementary

Time
30 minutes

Preparation
one photocopy of worksheet A and one photocopy of worksheet B for each pair

Warm-up

❶ Write the following activities on pieces of paper: *doing homework, riding a bicycle, driving a car, using a computer, cleaning a window*. Fold them up. Invite a student to come to the front and choose one.

❷ Ask the student to mime the activity and ask the others to guess what he/she is doing, using his/her real name, e.g. *Sophie is doing homework. Nathan is riding a bicycle.* When someone has guessed correctly also elicit what he/she is wearing, e.g. *She's wearing a dress. He's wearing trousers and a shirt.*

❸ Repeat by inviting other students to the front. You may wish to write useful words on the board. Make sure they are familiar with all the key vocabulary.

Main activity

❶ Divide the class into pairs. Hand out an A and a B worksheet to each pair. They must not look at their partner's worksheet.

❷ Explain that although their pictures are very similar, there are 12 differences. Point out one difference by asking an A student to say what James is doing and wearing, and whether his hair is long or short. Then ask a B student to do the same. The class tells you what the difference is.

❸ Tell students that they have to find 12 differences between the people in their two pictures. They also have to find one person who is the same in both pictures.

❹ Students take it in turns to ask each other questions about their pictures. They should ask questions about what each person is doing and wearing and whether he/she has got long or short hair. Tell them to make a note of the differences. Set a time limit of fifteen minutes for this activity.

❺ When they have finished, students then compare their pictures. Ask them to report to the class the differences they found.

Answers
1 James is wearing glasses in A, but in B he's wearing a baseball cap.
2 Karen is wearing a dress in A, but in B she's wearing jeans and a T-shirt.
3 Charlotte is playing a computer game in A, but in B she's watching TV.
4 Daniel is playing the guitar in A, but in B he's singing.
5 Daniel isn't wearing sunglasses in A, but in B he's wearing sunglasses.
6 Chloe is singing in A, but in B she's playing the guitar.
7 Chloe has got short hair in A, but in B she's got long hair.
8 Patrick and Katie are talking in A, but in B they're dancing.
9 Patrick is wearing shorts in A, but in B he's wearing jeans.
10 Katie is wearing a skirt and a T-shirt in A, but in B she's wearing a dress.
11 Claire and Isobel are dancing in A, but in B they're talking.
12 Isobel is wearing a dress in A, but in B she's wearing jeans and a T-shirt.
The person who does not change is Chris. He's doing the same thing and wearing the same clothes in A and B.

Follow-up

○ Divide students into pairs. Give the pairs pictures from a magazine. The pictures should show people doing things. Each pair writes a brief description of the picture they have, but they should deliberately include several false details. They should then exchange pictures and texts with another pair. Their task is to read the text and find the differences between the picture and its description.

A

Look at the picture. What are the people doing? What are they wearing? Have they got long or short hair?
Describe your picture to your partner and listen to your partner's description.
Find 12 differences. There is one person who is the same in both pictures. Who is it?

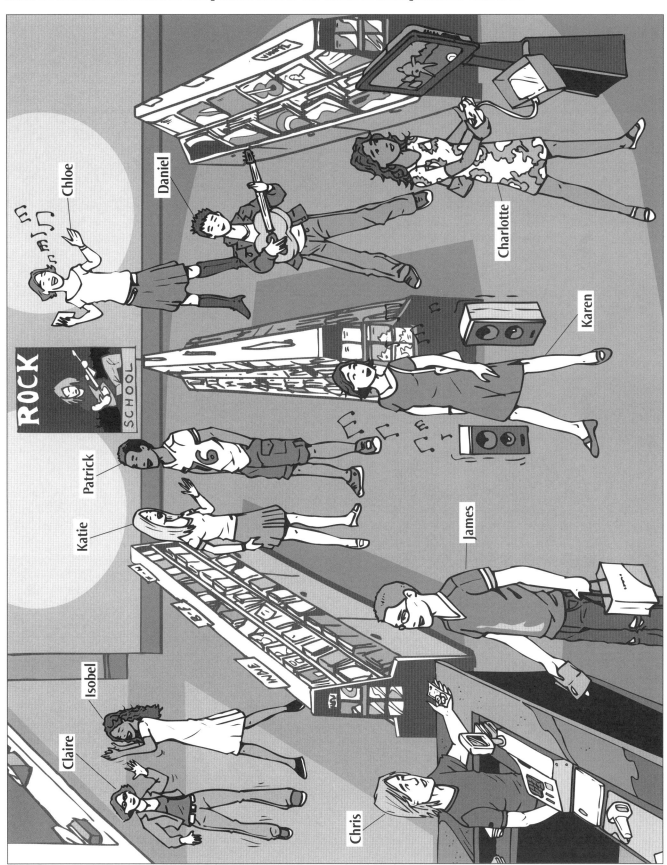

B

Look at the picture. What are the people doing? What are they wearing? Have they got long or short hair?
Describe your picture to your partner and listen to your partner's description.
Find 12 differences. There is one person who is the same in both pictures. Who is it?

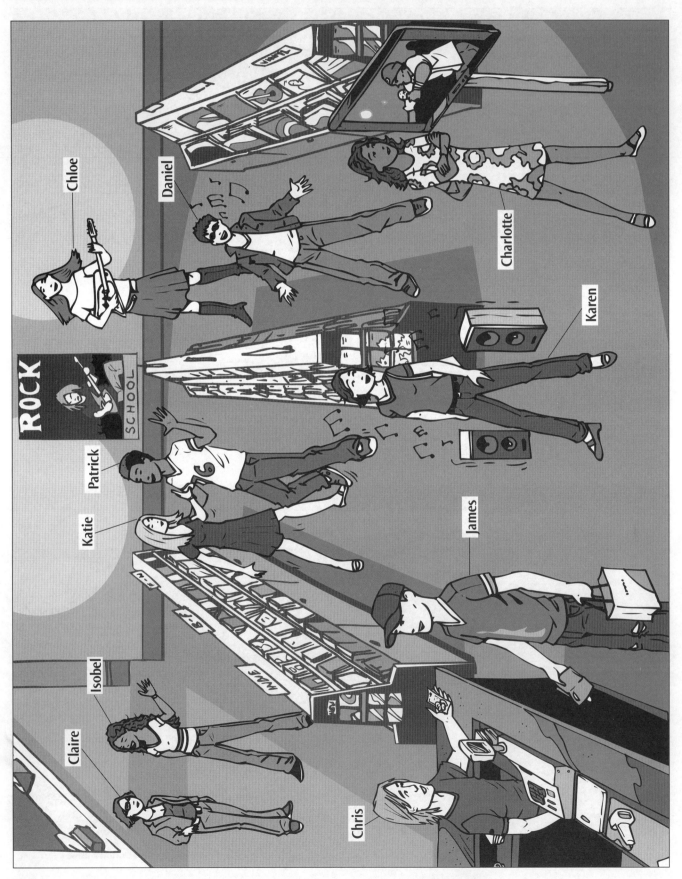

What can it describe?

Language focus
adjectives

Key vocabulary
adjectives from the puzzle; *clue*, *crossword puzzle*

Skills focus
writing and speaking: defining adjectives

Level
intermediate

Time
30–40 minutes

Preparation
one photocopy each of worksheet A for half of the class and one photocopy each of worksheet B for the other half of the class

Extra notes
Dictionaries would be useful for this activity.

Warm-up

❶ Introduce the idea of guessing adjectives by giving examples like these: *This adjective can describe a fire or the weather on a sunny day.* (hot) *This describes someone who doesn't like talking to strangers. It can only describe a person.* (shy)

❷ Choose students to make similar sentences about other adjectives for the rest of the class. The others guess the answers.

Main activity

❶ Explain to students that they are going to complete a crossword puzzle. Divide the class into two halves and put them on different sides of the classroom. Give one half the A worksheets, and the other half the B worksheets. All the A students should work in pairs or groups of three, likewise the B students.

❷ Tell pairs/groups to look at all the words in their half of the puzzle and check that they know what they mean. They have to decide together how they are going to explain the words to the other students without saying the actual words.

❸ Each student should write the clues on his/her worksheet. When students are confident that they understand the words and can describe them, reorganise the class into pairs with one A and one B student in each pair. They must not look at their partner's worksheet.

❹ Students take it in turns to ask for definitions, e.g. *What's number 4?* If they have problems guessing the word, their partner should help them by saying the first letter, then the second letter, etc. Set a time limit of 20 minutes.

❺ At the end, students compare worksheets and see if their words are correct. Find out how successful they were.

Follow-up

○ Choose a passage from a reader at the students' level. Copy the passage but remove all the adjectives. Ask students to fill in the missing adjectives (you can either give them a list of the adjectives you have removed, or leave the choice of adjectives entirely up to them). When they have finished they look at the original passage and compare it with theirs. Has their use of adjectives made the story different?

○ Ask students to write a short story using as many of the adjectives from the puzzle as possible.

A

Look at the words in your crossword puzzle.
You will need to help your partner guess the
words. Write clues under the puzzle to explain
what each word means and what it describes.

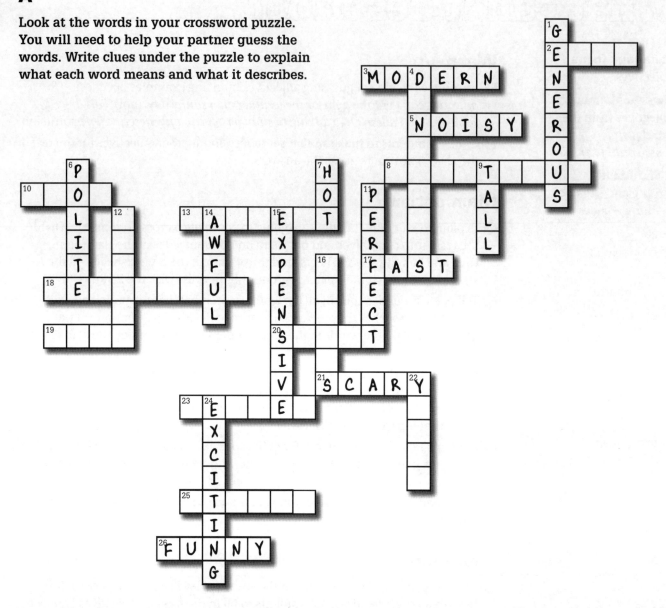

1 <u>This describes someone who likes giving things to others. It usually describes a person.</u>

3 ....

5 ....

6 ....

7 ....

9 ....

11 ....

14 ....

15 ....

17 ....

21 ....

24 ....

26 ....

B

Look at the words in your crossword puzzle.
You will need to help your partner guess the
words. Write clues under the puzzle to explain
what each word means and what it describes.

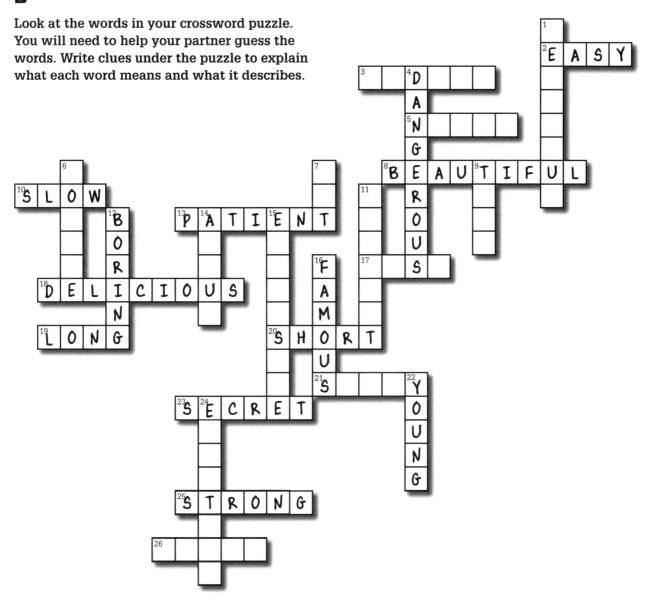

2 This describes something that is not difficult. It can describe a question in a test.

4 ....

8 ....

10 ....

12 ....

13 ....

16 ....

18 ....

19 ....

20 ....

22 ....

23 ....

25 ....

Guess what it is

Language focus
present simple; present simple passive

Key vocabulary
household objects and machines; *alarm clock, credit card, headphones, light bulb, microphone, tin opener*;
a kind of, like, similar to, something you use for

Skills focus
speaking: explaining what things are and what they are used for

Level
upper-intermediate

Time
20–30 minutes

Preparation
one photocopy for each group of 3 or 4 students, cut into separate cards

Extra notes
You may want to revise adjectives of shape before doing this activity.

Warm-up

❶ Think of a classroom object, e.g. *stapler* or *pencil case*. Describe it without naming it and ask students to guess what it is. Use phrases like *It's something you use for …*, *It's a kind of …*, *It's similar to …*, *It's very popular with teenagers …* Repeat with other objects in the classroom or in the home. You may want to write useful phrases on the board.

❷ Invite students to think of more objects and describe them to the class, without using the word itself. Point out that they are not allowed to use their hands or mime to help them. The others try to guess the object.

Main activity

❶ Divide the class into groups of three or four. Hold up a set of cards and explain that on each card there is a picture of an object with its name. They describe it to their group, *without* saying the name (or any part of the name) of the object and without using the two words at the bottom of each card. Demonstrate with one of the cards. Emphasise that miming or gesturing is not permitted.

❷ Students take turns to select a card from the pile and describe the object to the others in their group. They must not show the card to anyone. The student who is the first to correctly guess the word keeps that card. The person with the most cards at the end of the activity is the winner. Set a time limit of 15 minutes for this.

❸ Extend the activity with the whole class by asking each student to write down a new object on a piece of paper (with two 'forbidden' words underneath). Swap the pieces of paper around, then choose students to describe the object on their paper and ask the class to guess what it is.

Follow-up

○ Students find unusual shots or close-ups of objects in magazines or on the Internet. They bring them in for other students to discuss using phrases like *It could be …*, *It looks like …*

○ Ask students to pick one of the cards and write an advertisement for that object. They should explain why it is useful and special, and try to make customers want to buy it, without actually using the name of the object. They can read out their adverts and ask the other students to guess what they are advertising.

MP3 player	car	guitar	coffee machine

music download	drive wheel	music play	drink hot

DVD player	motorbike	washing machine	bicycle

film movie	fast scooter	clothes clean	ride cycle

tennis racket	camera	mirror	alarm clock

play ball	computer photo	look reflection	wake up time

fridge	microphone	mobile phone	rucksack
food cold	sing music	call text	carry back

book	credit card	watch	television

read story	pay plastic	time clock	watch programme

laptop	light bulb	microwave	headphones

Internet computer	light electricity	cook fast	listen music

My perfect friend

Language focus
present simple
statements; *and, but,
because*

Key vocabulary
*interests, laugh, perfect,
poem, tell the truth*

Skills focus
writing and speaking:
expressing opinions;
describing a friend

Level
elementary

Time
45 minutes

Preparation
one photocopy for each
student

Extra notes
It would be useful to
write a copy of the poem
on the board before the
lesson, with the gaps left
empty to fill in together.
If possible, cover this up
until you need it.

Warm-up

❶ Brainstorm words connected with friendship and write a list on the board, e.g. *friendly, like, talk, text, best friend, secret, Internet, laugh, have fun, go out.*

❷ Ask students if they have a *perfect friend.*

Main activity

❶ Tell students they are going to discuss ideas about friendship. Hand out the worksheets. With the whole class, look at the ten statements, making sure that they understand what each one means.

❷ Students think about the statements, decide whether they are true or false for themselves and tick the boxes. When they have completed the questionnaire individually, put them in pairs to discuss their answers.

❸ Encourage students to provide more information about their answers by using sentences such as *I often phone my friends after school because we talk about homework* or *I don't often phone my friends after school because it's expensive.* Their partner asks follow-up questions, e.g. *Do you often phone them at the weekend?*

❹ Choose one or two students to share their answers with the whole class. Invite follow-up questions.

❺ Tell students that they are going to write a poem in pairs about what makes a perfect friend. As an example, use the outline on the worksheet to complete a poem together on the board, e.g.
My perfect friend listens when I feel sad.
And laughs when I feel happy.
My perfect friend sometimes forgets my sister's name
But he never forgets my birthday.
My perfect friend plays football like Lionel Messi.
And dances like Justin Timberlake.
He is funny and intelligent.
My perfect friend drinks apple juice and eats spaghetti.
He loves films but hates homework.
He's my perfect friend because he's always kind.

❻ Explain to students that they should complete their poem using the types of words indicated in brackets. The poem can be about a real or an imaginary friend. Encourage students to be creative.

❼ When students have finished, choose some of them to read out their poems to the whole class.

Follow-up

○ Ask students to write something about a friend on his/her social networking site on the Internet. They should tell the person why they like being their friend.

○ Ask them to choose a celebrity from their own country or of world renown and write a paragraph explaining why they would like to be his/her friend.

1 Are these statements true or false?

		T	F
1	I often phone my friends after school.	☐	☐
2	I meet my friends at the weekend.	☐	☐
3	I've got some friends from other schools.	☐	☐
4	I like the same music as my friends.	☐	☐
5	I always tell the truth to my friends.	☐	☐
6	My best friend lives near me.	☐	☐
7	I often go to the cinema with my friends.	☐	☐
8	I never get angry with my friends.	☐	☐
9	I think it's important to have the same interests as my friends.	☐	☐
10	I have friends on the Internet.	☐	☐

Discuss your answers with a partner.

2 What makes a perfect friend? Complete this poem with your partner.

My perfect friend, by _____

My perfect friend listens when I _____ (verb),

And laughs when I _____ (verb).

My perfect friend sometimes _____ (verb),

But he/she never _____ (verb).

My perfect friend _____ (verb) like _____ (famous person 1),

And _____ (verb) like _____ (famous person 2).

He/She is _____ (adjective) and _____ (adjective).

My perfect friend drinks _____ (drink) and eats _____ (food).

He/She loves _____ (noun) but hates _____ (noun).

He's/She's my perfect friend because _____

_____ (finish the sentence).

Now compare your poem with another pair's poem. Are any of your ideas the same?

The best of friends

Language focus
present simple; present perfect; *should*

Key vocabulary
easy-going, friendship, generous, good-looking, kind, loyal, patient, popular, relax, similar to, spend time

Skills focus
speaking: discussing friendship; giving advice

Level
intermediate

Time
45–60 minutes

Preparation
one photocopy for each student

Extra notes
Dictionaries would be useful for this activity.

Warm-up

1 Prompt the class to give you ways of expressing opinions, agreeing and disagreeing. You may want to put these phrases on the board:
*In my opinion … I think that … From my point of view … For me …
I agree. That's right. You're right. I think the same.
I don't really agree. I completely disagree. I don't think that's right.*

2 Brainstorm adjectives connected with friendship. During this activity, introduce the adjectives from the key vocabulary.

Main activity

1 Divide the class into pairs and hand out a worksheet to each student. Together they look at the attributes of a friend.

2 They discuss the attributes and decide which are the most important and which are the least important. Encourage them to use the language of opinions, agreeing and disagreeing. Set a time limit of ten minutes for this.

3 Reorganise the pairs into groups of three or four, and ask them to compare their lists. Groups report back to the class on their findings.

4 Students stay in groups but work individually to read the statements about friendship and decide whether they agree with, disagree with or are not sure about each one.

5 In their group, students discuss their opinions about the statements and justify their viewpoints. They can try to change each other's opinions but do not need to reach a group decision about each statement.

6 Students read the letters individually. Then they decide in groups what advice Sara should give the two teenagers. What do they think would be the best solution to the problem? Encourage students to use *should* and *shouldn't*.

Follow-up

○ Students write a reply from Sara, giving advice to either Emily or Olivia. They use the worksheet letters as a model.

○ Students role play a discussion between Emily and Olivia about the problem. Allow some time for them to make notes for this.

○ Students write a description of their real or imaginary best friend, explaining why they are such a good friend.

1 What is important in a friend? With a partner, rank the adjectives from 1 (most important) to 10 (least important). If you don't agree, try to persuade your partner to change his/her mind.

easy-going ☐   generous ☐

funny ☐   good-looking ☐

clever ☐   full of ideas ☐

kind ☐   loyal ☐

patient ☐   popular ☐

2 Do you agree or disagree with these statements? Circle ☺ if you agree, ☹ if you disagree or 😐 if you're not sure. Then discuss your opinions in a group.

1 It's better to have one or two good friends than a lot of friends. ☺ ☹ 😐
2 I prefer spending time with friends to spending time with my family. ☺ ☹ 😐
3 I think I'll have the same friends in ten years' time. ☺ ☹ 😐
4 My friends are very similar to me. ☺ ☹ 😐
5 If I tell my friends a secret, they won't tell other people. ☺ ☹ 😐
6 It's important to see your friends often. ☺ ☹ 😐

3 Read these two letters to a problem page. What would your advice be to Emily and Olivia? Discuss your answers in groups.

Dear Sara,

I've been best friends with Olivia for years. We do everything together and we always have a really good time. I don't have many friends, but I think that isn't a problem because Olivia is such a good friend. But now Olivia doesn't want to spend as much time with me as before. She sometimes goes to the cinema or to other people's houses and she doesn't invite me. I've sent her text messages at weekends to ask if she wants to meet, but she doesn't text back. What should I do? I don't want to argue with Olivia, but she doesn't seem interested in our friendship.

Please help,

Emily

Dear Sara,

I've been best friends with Emily for the last two or three years, but now I've started to spend more time with other people. I haven't stopped being friends with Emily, but I sometimes find it difficult that she wants to spend all of her time with me – I want to see other people too, and relax in different ways. The problem is, I don't think Emily likes my other friends, so if I go out with them, I can't invite her. I feel bad at weekends when I don't see Emily, but I want to spend time with my other friends as well.

What should I do?

Olivia

Friendship

Language focus
question forms (present simple, present perfect, second conditional)

Key vocabulary
cheerful, energetic, enthusiastic, generous, honest, individual, loyal, optimistic, sensible, sociable, sympathetic, thoughtful, tolerant, trustworthy, warm

Skills focus
writing and speaking: creating and conducting a survey; summarising information

Level
upper-intermediate

Time
40–50 minutes

Preparation
one photocopy for each student

Extra notes
This activity works best with a higher level class. Dictionaries may be useful for this activity.

Warm-up

❶ Ask students to think of one adjective each that describes someone they like. Write all of their suggestions on the board.

❷ Then ask them to say which of the adjectives on the board describes the quality they value most in a friend.

Main activity

❶ Hand out the worksheets and check comprehension of the adjectives from the list at the top. You may want to hand out dictionaries at this stage.

❷ Divide the class into groups of three or four students. Explain that they are going to make a questionnaire to survey the class on the topic of friendship.

❸ Focus on the two questions given as examples. Point out that these are designed to find out how *loyal* people are to their friends.

❹ Ask groups to consider the other adjectives listed and to choose five more from the box that best describe a good friend. Their opinions will probably differ, so they will need to negotiate.

❺ Tell groups that they should now make two survey questions for each of the adjectives they have chosen. They will need to form questions that can be answered with a number on a scale from 0 (= never) to 4 (= always). Give examples of question types: *Are you …? Do you …? Have you ever …? Would you ever …? If … , would you …?*

❻ Give groups 15–20 minutes to work out their ten questions. All members of the group should write these on their own worksheet.

❼ Students mingle and ask their questions – they should have time to interview three to five people. They record the answers by ticking the appropriate box. They may end up with several ticks in each box. Encourage them to ask follow-up questions and to use the back of the worksheet to note down interesting or typical answers.

❽ Groups reassemble to collate and discuss their results.

❾ Finally, each group reports on the results of their survey. They should make general observations (e.g. *Most people in the class are quite loyal to their friends …*) rather than comments on individuals.

Follow-up

◯ Ask groups to read out their most interesting or controversial question from their survey. Open these questions up for class discussion.

◯ With the class, compile a list of adjectives describing qualities that harm or destroy friendships (e.g. *jealous, bad-tempered, selfish*, etc.). Invite discussion as students make suggestions.

(loyal) trustworthy sociable
honest energetic thoughtful sensible
funny sympathetic warm individual patient
generous cheerful optimistic tolerant
enthusiastic brave

Key
0 = never   1 = rarely
2 = sometimes   3 = often
4 = always

Quality	Questions	0	1	2	3	4
LOYAL	1 Would you ever report a friend to a teacher or parent for doing something wrong?					
	2 Do you always support your friends in an argument?					
	3					
	4					
	5					
	6					
	7					
	8					
	9					
	10					
	11					
	12					

Nature game

Language focus
adjectives; present simple; *can, have got*

Key vocabulary
bat, elephant, giraffe, horse, kangaroo, lion, mouse, penguin, rabbit, shark, spider, tiger; beach, desert, field, forest, island, mountain, river, sea

Skills focus
speaking: describing features of the natural world

Level
elementary

Time
20–25 minutes

Preparation
one photocopy for each group of 3 or 4 students; a dice for each group; coins or counters to move around the board; a photocopy of the Rules for each group (optional)

Warm-up

❶ Brainstorm names of animals. Then do the same for geographical features (*river, lake, mountain, hill, valley, sea, beach*, etc.).

❷ Write one example from each category on the board (e.g. *bear, hill*), avoiding words that appear in the game. Invite students to make true statements using the singular or plural form, e.g. *Bears live in the forest. A bear can climb trees. There are lots of hills in San Francisco. A hill is smaller than a mountain.* Encourage them to use a range of verbs, e.g. *be, can* + verb, *have got, live, eat, run, fly, swim, hunt, sleep.* You may want to write these verbs on the board.

Main activity

❶ Divide the class into groups of three or four. Hand out a copy of the game board and a dice to each group. Tell students to place their coin or counter on START.

❷ Explain the rules of the game – see the Rules box below.

❸ Give students a few minutes to study the game board. Ask them to think of some sentences they can make using the words or describing the animals in the pictures. They can use either singular or plural forms.

❹ Students take it in turns to roll the dice and play the game.

Follow-up

⭕ Ask students to use two or more words/phrases from the game board to form sentences with *and, but* and *because*. They could do this in their groups, or you could elicit suggestions from the whole class. Examples:
Penguins swim in the sea and (they) eat fish.
Australia is an island and it's got lots of nice beaches.
Bats have got big ears, but they've got small eyes.
A mouse is a small animal, but it can move/run very fast.
Sharks are dangerous because they sometimes attack people.
Elephants don't live in the desert because they need lots of water.

⭕ Ask students to write ten true sentences about an animal of their choice from the game board. They can use the Internet to find or check information. In class, they form groups with others who have chosen the same animal and share their information. Invite groups to tell the rest of the class some of their most interesting pieces of information.

Rules for Nature game

1 Take it in turns to throw the dice. When you land on a square, make a true sentence using the words given or describing the animal. You cannot repeat information that another player has given before.

2 The other players decide if your sentence is true. (If there is any disagreement, ask the teacher.) If the sentence is false or repeats someone's information, you must go back two spaces.

3 The first player to reach FINISH is the winner.

From *Pairwork and Groupwork* © Cambridge University Press 2009 **PHOTOCOPIABLE**

10.1 Nature game

START · eat meat · forest · long legs · river · fast · mountain · dangerous · beach · wings · swim · island · intelligent · small · big ears · fly · desert · field · a long tail · sea · FINISH

Quick descriptions

Language focus
present simple;
adjectives

Key vocabulary
animals; animal
characteristics; natural
phenomena

Skills focus
speaking: describing
appearance,
characteristics and
habits

Level
intermediate

Time
30 minutes

Preparation
one photocopy for each
group of 4 students, cut
into cards; a photocopy
of the Rules for each
group (optional)

Extra notes
If some cards contain
words that are
unfamiliar to your
students, remove them
from the packs that you
hand out.

Warm-up

❶ On the board, write some example cards similar to those on the worksheet.
They should be to do with animals, plants or features of the natural world, e.g.

| a donkey | teeth | trees | a lake |

Elicit sentences to describe each of these things as clearly as possible, e.g. *It's an animal. It looks like a small horse but it's got long ears. People ride it or use it to carry things. / These things are in an animal's mouth. They are white and strong. The animal uses them to bite and eat food.*

❷ Think of a new example, e.g. *snake*, and describe it for the class to guess. Then invite a student to do the same.

Main activity

❶ Divide the class into groups of four. Split each group into an A pair and a B pair. Seat each group at a table with partners facing each other.

❷ Hand out the cards. Tell students to put them face down in a pile on the table.

❸ Explain the rules of the game – see the Rules box below. Choose one person from each group to keep the scores.

❹ Set a time limit of 20 minutes to play the game. At the end, find out which pair scored the highest number of points in the class.

Follow-up

○ Ask groups to think of three more nouns like those on the cards. They work together to write the clearest description they can think of for each one, using no more than two sentences. In turn, groups read out their descriptions to the class. The other students write down what they think the answers are.

○ Students work in pairs. Ask them to lay out the cards in front of them and to write sentences containing either two or three of the nouns on the cards. They can use the nouns in the singular or plural form. A sentence with two nouns scores one point and a sentence with three nouns scores five points. Set a time limit of ten minutes for the activity. At the end, pairs exchange sentences with another pair and they mark each other's work. Ask the pair with the highest score to read out their sentences. Then invite other pairs to read out their best sentence.

Rules for Quick descriptions

1   If you are the first player in pair A, take a card and describe the thing on it. You cannot say its name (or any part of its name) and you cannot use your hands to help you. Your partner has 30 seconds to listen and guess the answer. A member of pair B will check the time and call out 'Time's up!' after 30 seconds. You must not show the card to the other players.

2   Your pair scores two points for a correct answer. If the answer is wrong, pair B has a chance to guess and scores one point if their answer is correct.

3   Then it is pair B's turn to take a card, describe and guess. The game continues like this. At the end, the pair with the most points wins.

From *Pairwork and Groupwork* © Cambridge University Press 2009 **PHOTOCOPIABLE**

---

a valley	dolphins	insects	a jungle
a goat	a nest	waves	nuts
wings	clouds	a shell	ants
a parrot	bushes	a bat	feathers
mammals	a koala	a spider's web	reptiles
grass	fur	a crocodile	a cliff
lizards	sand	leaves	bears
a waterfall	a hippo	a cave	a bird's egg

The power of nature

Language focus
present simple; present passive

Key vocabulary
avalanche, blizzard, earthquake, flood, forest fire, hurricane, iceberg, landscape, landslide, lightning, mud, natural disaster, rainbow, sunlight, thunder, tornado, tsunami, volcano

Skills focus
writing and speaking: describing characteristics; making factual explanations

Level
upper-intermediate

Time
40 minutes

Preparation
one photocopy for each pair, cut into A and B parts

Extra notes
Dictionaries would be useful for this activity.

Warm-up

● Briefly revise words for natural disasters and extreme weather. Elicit the words by naming places or things famously associated with them, e.g. *Pompei* (volcano), *the Titanic* (iceberg), *New Orleans, 2005* (hurricane, flood), *the Indian Ocean, 2004* (tsunami, earthquake), *San Francisco, 1906* (earthquake, fire), *Antarctica* (blizzard).

Main activity

❶ Put students in pairs and hand out an A and a B worksheet to each pair. Students must not look at their partner's worksheet.

❷ Explain that each student has half of the puzzle filled in. They need to help their partner to fill in the other half by giving definitions of their words. They cannot say the word or any part of it – for example, in a definition for *thunderstorm*, they could not use the word *thunder* or *storm*.

❸ Give students five minutes to think about the words in their half of the puzzle and to check meanings or pronunciation in a dictionary if necessary. They should *not* write down the dictionary definitions.

❹ Students take it in turns to ask for definitions (*What's number 1?* etc.) and fill in the missing words. If they can't guess a word, advise them to leave it aside and return to it later. If they still can't think of it, their partner should give them the answer.

❺ When they have finished, students compare puzzles and check their spelling.

❻ Ask students to focus on the natural disasters in the puzzle. In their pairs, they select three of these disasters and work on the questions on their worksheet. Ask them to try to arrive at clear and accurate explanations/answers, which they should write down. They can consult other pairs for information if necessary.

❼ With the whole class, ask students to compare and discuss their answers to the questions.

Follow-up

○ Ask pairs to make their own crossword puzzle using about ten new words from the natural world. Tell them to draw the puzzle again as an empty grid and to write clues. They then swap with another pair and try to solve the puzzle they receive. At the end, they give feedback to the pair who wrote it, checking answers, commenting on the accuracy of the clues and pointing out any problems or difficulties.

○ Ask students to write an entry on one of the words in the puzzle for a website on the natural world. They should explain what the phenomenon is and what causes it, including examples if they wish. They can do some research for this on the Internet.

A

Discussion: Choose three of the natural disasters in the puzzle.
- How is each one caused?
- How is the landscape affected?
- How are people affected?

B

Discussion: Choose three of the natural disasters in the puzzle.
- How is each one caused?
- How is the landscape affected?
- How are people affected?

Our ideal timetable

Language focus
time; *on* + day; *at* + time

Key vocabulary
school subjects; days of
the week

Skills focus
speaking: talking about
activities on a timetable;
expressing opinions

Level
elementary

Time
25 minutes

Preparation
one photocopy for each
student

Warm-up

❶ Briefly revise school subjects by asking questions, e.g. *What's your favourite subject? What subject did you have before this lesson? What do you have next / after lunch / on Friday afternoons?*

❷ Write these sentence openings on the board: *I think …, I want (to) …, We should …* Ask the class: *Imagine you can change one thing in our school – what change do you want to make?* Give students a few minutes to discuss this in pairs or small groups, using the sentence openings on the board to help them. Then elicit a range of suggestions from the class. Ask for reasons or further information and invite others to say if they agree or disagree.

Main activity

❶ Put students in pairs and hand out a worksheet to each student.

❷ Explain that they are going to make an ideal school timetable for the week. They must include at least six subjects and at least one sport. However, it is up to them to decide what happens when. Remind them to use *on* with days of the week and *at* with times.

❸ Ask pairs to complete the table at the top of the worksheet. Students will need to negotiate with their partner to reach agreement.

❹ Now pairs discuss and fill in each day's timetable, including times for lessons and breaks. They can use one worksheet as a rough working plan and then write their final version on the second sheet.

❺ While they are working, draw five blank timetables in a row across the board.

❻ Ask students from five different pairs to come to the board. Assign one day of the week to each student and ask them to fill in their timetable for that day. Invite questions and comments from the rest of the class.

Follow-up

○ Ask pairs to write their five-day timetable clearly on a large piece of paper or cardboard. Display these on the wall and allow students to walk round and read each other's timetables. At the end, have a vote on which timetables are the most sensible, the most enjoyable and the most unusual.

○ For a quick listening exercise, draw the timetable below on the board and ask students to copy it down. Then read out the sentences in the box. Students listen and write the correct school subjects in the timetable.

9.00–9.50		At midday we were studying a map of South America. We were drawing and painting at ten to two. At twenty past nine we were learning about ancient Greece. We were acting in a play just after the morning break. At ten a.m. we were doing an experiment in the lab. We were playing basketball in the gym at quarter to three.
9.50–10.40		
10.40–11.00	Break	
11.00–11.50		
11.50–12.40		
12.40–1.40	Lunch	
1.40–2.30		
2.30–3.20		

Answers
9.00–9.50: history   9.50–10.40: science   11.00–11.50: drama
11.50–12.40: geography   1.40–2.30: art   2.30–3.20: PE

Subjects – six or more: ....

....

Sport(s) – one or more: ....

Other activities: ....

....

Break time(s): .... Lunch time: ....

MONDAY

Time	Subject/Activity

TUESDAY

Time	Subject/Activity

WEDNESDAY

Time	Subject/Activity

THURSDAY

Time	Subject/Activity

FRIDAY

Time	Subject/Activity

Finish the sentence

Language focus
modals: *should, must, ought to, have to*;
verb + infinitive with *to*

Key vocabulary
school subjects; *be allowed to, facilities, hit, make trouble, provide, smoke, uniform*

Skills focus
reading and speaking: forming sentences; giving reasons for opinions

Level
intermediate

Time
20–25 minutes

Preparation
one photocopy of both sets of cards (pages 75 and 76) for each group of 3 or 4 students, cut into separate cards; a photocopy of the Rules for each group (optional)

Warm-up

● Write the following sentence openings on the board: *Teachers should …, Schools must …, We all ought …, Everyone wants …, Most people need …* Elicit possible endings. Make sure that students can distinguish between the verbs which are followed by the infinitive + *to* and those without *to*.

Main activity

❶ Divide the class into groups of three or four and seat each group around a table.

❷ Hand out the 12 sentence opening cards to each group. Groups place these face down in a pile in the middle of their table without looking at them.

❸ Hand out the sentence ending cards, face down. Ask one student from each group to deal these out so that each player has several cards. In a group of four, students will have four cards each. In a group of three, they will have five cards with one left unused.

❹ Explain the rules of the game – see the Rules box below.

❺ Groups play the game. If one group finishes early, they can shuffle the cards and play again. They must not repeat any sentences that were made in the first round.

Answers
(The following are suggested possible answers. Other answers are also possible but unlikely – whether they are acceptable to the group will depend on the speaker's persuasiveness in giving reasons.)

A 2, 3, 6, 9	**D** 4, 5, 7, 10, 15	**G** 2, 3, 6, 12	**J** 3, 11, 16
B 2, 6, 9, 12, 13	**E** 3, 11, 16	**H** 1, 8, 9, 13, 16	**K** 4, 5, 7, 10, 15
C 1, 6, 11, 16	**F** 4, 5, 7, 10, 14, 15	**I** 4, 5, 7, 10, 14, 15	**L** 1, 8, 9, 13, 16

Follow-up

○ Ask groups to match the cards to form the best possible 12 sentences – that is, both grammatically correct and forming opinions that they agree with. (Four endings will be left unused.) Choose one group to read out their sentences. If others disagree with any of the opinions, open the issue for class discussion.

○ Ask students to choose one of the sentences made with the cards and to write an entry on this issue for a school website.

Rules for Finish the sentence

1 The first player turns over a card from the pile on the table and reads out the sentence opening.

2 Everyone looks for a suitable card in their hand to complete the sentence. If you are the first player to put down a card, you must read out the full sentence and give a good reason to support this opinion.

3 The others decide if your sentence is grammatically correct and if your reason is a good one. If not, you must pick up your card again and someone else can put down a card to complete the sentence. If there is disagreement, ask your teacher.

4 The first player to use up all their cards wins the game.

From *Pairwork and Groupwork* © Cambridge University Press 2009 **PHOTOCOPIABLE**

Sentence openings

A	B	C
We should …	Students shouldn't …	Teachers should …
D	**E**	**F**
Everyone needs …	Schools must …	Students ought …
G	**H**	**I**
All students should …	Teachers should never …	Students need …
J	**K**	**L**
Schools should …	Nobody wants …	Teachers should be allowed to …

Sentence endings

1 give us homework during the holidays.	**2** have to learn a foreign language at school.	**3** have good sports facilities.	**4** to learn maths at school.
5 to do homework every night.	**6** have to wear a school uniform.	**7** to study at the weekend.	**8** hit students.
9 go out of school during the lunch break.	**10** to study history at school.	**11** provide computers in every classroom.	**12** be allowed to leave school when they are 15.
13 smoke at school.	**14** to get hot lunches which are cooked at the school.	**15** to study hard before exams.	**16** send students home if they make trouble.

Leaving school

Language focus
mixed tenses; modals

Key vocabulary
language connected with
education and work

Skills focus
speaking: expressing
opinions; agreeing and
disagreeing

Level
upper-intermediate

Time
30 minutes

Preparation
one or more photocopies
of the worksheets (pages
78 and 79) to allow one
set of role cards for each
group of 3 or 4 students,
cut into separate cards

Extra notes
This activity is probably
best suited to older
teens. In a class of fewer
than 16 students, not
all the role cards will be
used; in a large class,
some groups will have
the same roles.

Warm-up

❶ Ask students to think of as many expressions as they can for stating an opinion, agreeing and disagreeing. Write these in three columns on the board.

❷ Make a controversial statement about education, e.g. *I think separate schools for boys and girls are better than mixed schools* or *In my opinion, all students should have to wear a school uniform.* Choose students to respond, alternately agreeing and disagreeing; and giving a reason. Some students may have to express an opinion that is not really their own, but this will be good practice for the role play.

Main activity

❶ Divide the class into groups of three or four students – four is the ideal number. Hand out a role card to each student, using role cards from the same set for each group.

❷ Explain the situation for the role play: *You are in a country where everyone must be 16 years old before they can leave school. There is now a new proposal from the government to change this leaving age from 16 to 18. Students will spend the last two years at an academic school or a college for job training.* Make sure that students understand the meaning of *proposal* and the concept of the minimum school leaving age. You may wish to summarise the proposal on the board.

❸ Tell students that they are going to have discussions where they act out the role of the person on their card. They should make arguments for or against the new proposal from this point of view.

❹ Give students a few minutes to read their card and prepare arguments for their role. Help them with any unknown vocabulary on their cards.

❺ Start the group discussion. Set a time limit of six minutes.

❻ Each group then joins up with another group who have a different set of role cards, and they discuss the issue again. You can walk round and join in the discussions, either speaking for yourself as a teacher or taking some other role. Set a time limit of eight minutes.

❼ With the whole class, ask students to summarise some of the arguments for and against the proposal. Which arguments did they find most convincing? What are their own real opinions? You could finish by taking a class vote on the proposal.

Follow-up

○ Ask students to do some research on the Internet to find out about the school leaving age in other countries. In the next lesson, students share and discuss their information.

○ In groups, students discuss other laws for young people in their country. For each of the following, what is the minimum legal age – and what age should it be? (You may need to check beforehand to be sure of the laws in your country.)

getting a driving licence	opening a bank account	working part-time
getting married	leaving home	working full-time
getting a passport	voting in elections	

Group A

✂

You are a 16-year-old student and you enjoy learning. You will stay at school until you are 18 and then go to university. You think this is important to have a good life in the future.	You are a parent with four children and you have a job. You want your children to get an education, but it is hard to find enough money to pay for all the things they need while they are at school.
You are a builder. You think the school leaving age should be lower, not higher. You believe that formal education is useless for lots of people and it would be better for them to learn 'on the job'.	You are the manager of a tourist business. You want motivated, intelligent employees and you would never choose people who leave school early.

Group B

✂

You are the manager of a group of shops and you don't agree with the proposal. You employ a lot of young people at the age of 16 because you don't have to pay them as much as older people.	You are a young teacher and you agree with the proposal. You believe that everyone should get a good education and that schools and colleges should provide interesting courses for everyone.
You are a police officer. You think the proposal is a good idea because it will keep young people busy and off the streets.	You are a 15-year-old student. You hate school and you want to get a job to earn money as soon as possible.

Group C

You are a social worker and you think the proposal is probably a good idea. You can see that at the moment too many young people leave education without qualifications and can't get a job.

You are an 18-year-old student. You think that it's a good idea to stay on at school, but you don't think people should have to do so.

You are a secondary school teacher. You are worried that the new proposal would mean more difficult students in your older classes.

You are a 30-year-old person working in a boring job from nine to five. For you, school days were the best time of your life. You don't think anyone should be in a hurry to leave school and join the 'rat race'.

Group D

You are a 16-year-old student and you disagree with the proposal. You will be glad when some students leave school at the end of this year because they cause trouble and make life difficult for those who want to learn.

You are a member of the government. You can see that most people in other countries are better educated than in yours. You want your country to be as successful as possible in a competitive world.

You are a 17-year-old factory worker. You are sorry you left school last year because your pay is low and you can see there isn't much chance of improving your position.

You are a successful farmer, managing a family farm. You left school when you were 16 and your son wants to do the same. You think another two years at school or college would be a waste of time.

World of sport

Language focus
present simple; gerunds

Key vocabulary
sports; *do athletics/ dancing/gymnastics*; *go cycling/running/ skateboarding/skiing/ snowboarding/ swimming*; *play basketball/football/ rugby/tennis/volleyball*

Skills focus
speaking: asking and answering questions about sports

Level
elementary

Time
20–30 minutes

Preparation
one photocopy for each group of 4 to 6 students, cut into picture cards and word cards; a photocopy of the Rules for each group (optional)

Extra notes
As these cards are reusable, it is a good idea to copy them onto different coloured cards so that you can easily separate them into sets.

Warm-up

❶ Brainstorm names of sports and compile a list on the board, including the key words. Ask whether we use each word with *play*, *do* or *go*. A general rule is that *play* is used for team games and *go* is used when the name of the sport ends in *-ing*. You may wish to add *play*, *do* and *go* to the sports on the board.

❷ Turn over a picture card and show it to the students. Ask the question suggested by the picture, e.g *Do you play tennis?* Turn over a word card and again display it. Answer the question according to the prompt, e.g. *No, I don't, I go jogging* or *Yes, I do* if the word card and picture card match.

❸ Invite a student to turn over a picture card and ask the corresponding question. Invite another student to turn over a word card and answer accordingly

Main activity

❶ Divide the class into groups of four to six. Each group has two teams seated on opposite sides of their table.

❷ Give each group a set of word cards and a set of picture cards. They spread the cards out face down on the table, the word cards on one side and the picture cards on the other. Make sure the picture cards and the word cards do not get mixed up.

❸ Explain the rules for the activity (see the Rules box below). Emphasise that in each round of the game, the first player turns over a picture card and the second player turns over a word card.

❹ Set a time limit of ten minutes to complete the game. If you wish, students can shuffle the cards and play again.

Follow-up

○ Ask students to write a paragraph about the sports or activities they do in their free time.

○ In groups, students prepare a new memory game using other verbs and pictures taken from magazines or the Internet, e.g. *cook, dance, sing, eat, drink, read*. This time the questions and answers should be in the present continuous, e.g. *Is she cooking? Yes, she is. / No, she isn't, she's dancing.*

Rules for World of sport

1 Divide into two teams and sit on opposite sides of the table.

2 A player from Team A turns over a picture card and asks a player from Team B a question, using the card, e.g. *Do you play football?*

3 The player from Team B turns over a word card and answers *Yes, I do* if the word is the same as the picture, or e.g. *No, I don't, I go cycling* if the word is different from the picture.

4 If the picture card and the word card are the same and they answer correctly, that team keeps the cards. If the word doesn't match the picture, the players turn both cards face down again.

5 When there are no more cards left, the team with the most cards wins.

From *Pairwork and Groupwork* © Cambridge University Press 2009 **PHOTOCOPIABLE**

---

		horse-riding	karate
		dancing	gymnastics
		tennis	swimming
		athletics	skiing
		snowboarding	basketball
		running	rugby
		football	skateboarding
		cycling	volleyball

Music and me

Language focus
present simple
questions; gerunds

Key vocabulary
types of music and
instruments

Skills focus
writing and speaking:
completing a
questionnaire;
expressing opinions

Level
intermediate

Time
30–45 minutes

Preparation
one photocopy for each
student

Extra notes
If you have time to
organise it, play a
popular song to start off
the lesson.

Warm-up

❶ Introduce the topic by asking students what songs or bands are popular at the moment. You could also ask them if they like to listen to any radio stations.

❷ Ask for examples of the different types of music mentioned in the questionnaire on the worksheet, e.g. *heavy metal, rock, rap*.

Main activity

❶ Hand out a worksheet to each student.

❷ Explain that they should think about their own musical tastes and complete the profile with true information. Allow students up to five minutes for this.

❸ Elicit the questions they need to obtain the same information from a partner. You may want to write these or prompts on the board. Invite students to ask you a few of the questions and give true answers about your own musical tastes. Suggested questions are:
What's your favourite kind of music?
Who's your favourite singer or band?
What song do you listen to when you're happy?
What do you think about dancing?
Do you have a favourite song at the moment?
How do you find out about music?
Is there a song you hate?
What's your favourite instrument?
Is there a singer or band you don't like?
When do you listen to music?
Do you download music or buy CDs?
Do you have a special song that reminds you of something?

❹ Divide students into pairs. Tell them to take it in turns to ask each other questions. Encourage them to ask follow-up questions.

❺ Students report back to the whole class by telling you anything interesting they have learnt about their partner's musical tastes.

❻ Ask students to look at the questionnaire. Tell them to think of a time when listening to music can help them, e.g. *going for a run*. Then ask them to think of a time when music is unhelpful or irritating, e.g. *trying to talk on the phone*. Ask them why listening to music is sometimes nice and sometimes not. What is the difference between *listening to* music and *hearing* music?

❼ They complete the questionnaire individually, then talk together in pairs about whether they like listening to music in each situation. They discuss what kind of music they think is best.

❽ Reorganise the pairs into groups of four. They discuss their answers to the questionnaire.

Follow-up

○ Ask students to make a profile of their favourite singer/band using magazines and the Internet. Encourage them to include photographs. Their finished work can be collected into a class music magazine or displayed on the wall.

○ Record ten brief excerpts from different kinds of music. Play them to the students and get them to discuss what they could be used for, e.g. what products they could advertise or what kind of films they would be good for.

1 Complete your music profile. Then talk about it with your partner.

1 My favourite kind of music is _____

2 My favourite singer/band is _____

3 A song I listen to when I'm happy is _____

4 I think dancing is _____

5 The song I really like at the moment is _____

6 I find out about music from _____

7 A song I hate is _____

8 My favourite instrument is _____

9 A singer/band I really don't like is _____

10 I always listen to music when _____

11 I get my music from _____

12 I like listening to _____ because it reminds me of

_____

2 Complete the questionnaire and then discuss your answers with your partner.

Do you like hearing music when you're doing these activities? If yes, what kind of music (e.g. *heavy metal, rock, rap, pop, electronic, jazz, classical*)?

1 Shopping for clothes   No ☐   Yes ☐   Kind of music: _____

2 Shopping for food   No ☐   Yes ☐   Kind of music: _____

3 Eating in a restaurant   No ☐   Yes ☐   Kind of music: _____

4 Eating at home   No ☐   Yes ☐   Kind of music: _____

5 Travelling by train   No ☐   Yes ☐   Kind of music: _____

6 Travelling by bike   No ☐   Yes ☐   Kind of music: _____

7 Waiting at the dentist's   No ☐   Yes ☐   Kind of music: _____

8 Doing exercise   No ☐   Yes ☐   Kind of music: _____

9 Doing homework   No ☐   Yes ☐   Kind of music: _____

10 Going to sleep   No ☐   Yes ☐   Kind of music: _____

Life of leisure

Language focus
language of opinions

Key vocabulary
appreciate, communicate, essential, gallery, individual, influence, judge, leisure, responsibility, spend time, taste

Skills focus
speaking: talking at length about leisure time; arguing a point

Level
upper-intermediate

Time
30–45 minutes

Preparation
one photocopy for each group of 3 or 4 students, cut into separate cards

Extra notes
This activity is useful practice for a speaking exam. Dictionaries may be useful for this activity.

Warm-up

❶ Write this statement on the board: *Teenagers have too much freedom.* Then add the following phrases underneath:
I totally agree/disagree with this statement.
In my opinion … I (don't) think … From my point of view, …
In some ways I agree that … It's (partly) true that …
However, … On the other hand, …
Talk about the statement for about half a minute, saying whether you agree or disagree with it, and expressing arguments for and against it. Use as many of the phrases above as you can.

❷ Ask students whether they agree or disagree with you. Encourage them to use the expressions on the board.

Main activity

❶ Divide students into groups of three or four. Hand out a set of cards to each group, placed face down in a pack on the table.

❷ The first student takes a card and reads out the statement to the group. He/she should aim to talk for about half a minute, following the example in the Warm-up. They will need up to 20 seconds to prepare themselves. Some students may find the activity hard to do at first but will find it easier as they get more practice. Tell them they don't have to say anything original or exciting, or worry about producing perfect language. If there are any words on the cards they are unfamiliar with, allow them to ask you for a definition or use a dictionary.

❸ When the student has finished his/her individual talk or has run out of things to say, the others join in by asking questions and expressing their own opinions. The whole group should join in the discussion. Remind them to use the phrases from the Warm-up.

❹ After a few minutes, the card is returned to the bottom of the pack and the next student takes a card. Set a time limit for the activity.

❺ Finish by asking which cards were the most interesting and discuss a few of those statements with the whole class.

Follow-up

○ Ask students to choose a card at random. They then write an argument for or against the statement, giving plenty of reasons and examples to back up their views.

○ Students make some similar cards about teenage life, school or parents, swap cards and play again in another lesson.

Teenagers don't read enough.	My free time would be different if I had more money.
It's essential to have a computer in your bedroom.	The best way to communicate is by texting.
Teenagers don't do enough exercise.	The Internet is the best way to find out the news.
My friends have a big influence on how I spend my time.	In 30 years' time, people won't read books.
Music is the most important thing in a teenager's life.	Watching TV together is a good family activity.
Parents don't appreciate our tastes in music and clothes.	Teenagers think free time is more important than anything else.
Museums and art galleries are boring.	Girls have more leisure time than boys.
Individual sports are better than team sports.	Going to the cinema is more fun than watching a DVD.
Going to a concert is more fun than going to the cinema.	You can judge people by their taste in music and clothes.
You should spend more time with your family than your friends.	Teenagers spend too much time shopping.

Press conference

Language focus
present simple; past
simple; present
continuous; *going to*

Key vocabulary
*actor, born, career, free
time, married, model,
star, success*

Skills focus
writing and speaking:
creating a profile; doing
an interview

Level
elementary

Time
35–45 minutes

Preparation
one photocopy and
a blank name label
for each student; a
magazine photo of a
glamorous-looking
person to use in the
Warm-up (optional)

Warm-up

❶ Copy the ten headings from the *My life as a star* section onto the board. Invent a name for a famous person, e.g. *Angelica Devine, singer*. If you have brought in a photo to represent this person, show it to the class.

❷ Ask students to help you fill in information about this person for the headings on the board. You may need to teach the words *career* and *success*. Make brief notes and draw attention to the tenses that are appropriate.

❸ Elicit questions for the headings, e.g. *When/where were you born? Where do you live now? Are you married? Have you got any children? What did you do before you were famous? How did your career begin? What was your biggest success last year? What do you do in your free time? Who are your friends? What are you doing at the moment? What are you going to do next year / in the future?* If your students are having trouble with these questions, write prompts on the board: *Where / born? How / career / begin?* etc. These questions do not need to be answered.

Main activity

❶ Divide the class into groups of three or four students and hand out the worksheets and name labels. Assign the following roles to the members of each group: *actor, pop star, sports star, model*. (For a group of three, use three of these.)

❷ Explain to students that they are each going to play the part of a famous person at a press conference with news reporters. First they need to make up a name for themselves. Tell them to write this and their profession on their name label so that others can see who they are.

❸ Give students five minutes to write notes in the top part of the worksheet. If they like, they can base their information on the life of a real person, but they should change names, dates and places.

❹ Students take it in turns to be interviewed in their celebrity role. The others take the role of reporters and make notes in the interview boxes on their worksheet. Set a time limit of four minutes for each interview. The reporters should try to get as much information as they can in this time. Ensure that all group members are involved in asking questions.

❺ With the whole class, ask different students to report on the information they got about one of the famous people they interviewed.

Follow-up

○ Ask groups to develop a fuller version of one of their press conferences, writing down the questions and answers as a script. You could suggest special occasions, e.g. before/after the MTV awards, before/after the Academy Awards in Hollywood, before/after the World Cup football competition. Give the groups time to practise and then ask them to perform for the class. You may be able to film the performances and play them back, inviting comments from the rest of the class after each one.

○ Ask students to choose one of the stars they interviewed and write an article on him/her for a fan website.

My life as a star

Born (date, place):

_____

Present home:

_____

Family (married? children?):

_____

_____

Before you were famous:

_____

_____

Beginning of career:

_____

_____

Biggest success last year:

_____

_____

Free-time activities:

_____

_____

Famous friends:

_____

_____

At the moment:

_____

_____

Future plans:

_____

_____

_____

Interview 1

Name: ....

....
....
....
....
....
....
....
....
....
....
....
....
....
....
....
....

Interview 2

Name: ....

....
....
....
....
....
....
....
....
....
....
....
....
....
....
....
....

Interview 3

Name: ....

....
....
....
....
....
....
....
....
....
....
....
....
....
....
....
....

Monroe and Chaplin

Language focus
past simple; past simple passive; past continuous

Key vocabulary
appearance, character, create, divorce, notice, photographer, role, screen test, serious, silent, sleeping tablet, weekly

Skills focus
reading and speaking: scanning a text for information; asking questions

Level
intermediate

Time
40–45 minutes

Preparation
one photocopy for each pair, cut into A and B parts; sticky labels with names of famous people for the Warm-up

Extra notes
Dictionaries would be useful for this activity.

Warm-up

❶ Stick a label with the name of a famous person on each student's back.

❷ Elicit some questions that students can ask the others to identify the person on their label, e.g. *Is the person a man or a woman? Is she alive now? Where is/was he from? What is/was her job? What does he look like? What films did she make / sport does he play (etc.)?*

❸ Students mingle, asking and answering. When they guess the name correctly, they remove their label but keep circulating to help others. Set a time limit of six or seven minutes for this activity.

Main activity

❶ Write the names *Marilyn Monroe* and *Charlie Chaplin* on the board. Ask students if they know who they both are. Don't go into details here.

❷ Put students in pairs and hand out an A and a B worksheet to each pair. Students must not look at their partner's worksheet.

❸ Ask students to read the first text on their sheet, checking vocabulary in a dictionary if necessary. If they have any problems with comprehension, they can ask you for help.

❹ Now ask them to read the second text and to think about questions they can ask to find out the missing information.

❺ Student A asks questions to complete the text on Charlie Chaplin. Then student B does the same to complete the text on Marilyn Monroe.

❻ At the end, each student reads out their completed text and their partner listens to check that the information is correct.

Follow-up

◯ Get one of Chaplin's films on DVD, e.g. *The Gold Rush*, *City Lights* or *Modern Times*. Select a sequence of about five minutes and play it for the class. In pairs, students recall and describe the action. With the whole class, ask questions, e.g. *What did he do when …? Why/How did he …? What happened after they …?*

◯ Find a recording of Elton John's tribute to Marilyn Monroe, *Candle in the Wind* (the 1974 version) and make copies of the lyrics. You will probably want to print the first two verses only, as the later verses may be inappropriate for your class. In pairs, students work through the lyrics, using dictionaries where necessary. Check comprehension with the class. Help them with the metaphors: 'They crawled out of the woodwork' probably refers to people from the film world and the media who were attracted, insect-like, to Marilyn's beauty. 'They set you on the treadmill' suggests a repetitive routine that she could not escape from. Finally, play the song for the class.

A

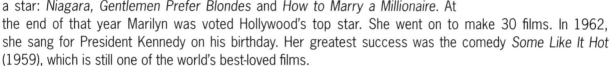

Marilyn Monroe was born as Norma Jeane Baker, in Los Angeles on 1st June 1926. In 1944 she was working in an aeroplane factory when she was noticed by a photographer, who helped her to become a model. In 1946 she had a screen test with the 20th Century Fox film studio and started using the name Marilyn Monroe. Her first film appearance was in 1947.

At first she had only small roles. But three big films in 1953 made her a star: *Niagara, Gentlemen Prefer Blondes* and *How to Marry a Millionaire*. At the end of that year Marilyn was voted Hollywood's top star. She went on to make 30 films. In 1962, she sang for President Kennedy on his birthday. Her greatest success was the comedy *Some Like It Hot* (1959), which is still one of the world's best-loved films.

But Marilyn felt that she was never seen as a serious actress and she did not find happiness in her personal life. She had three husbands, including baseball star Joe DiMaggio and writer Arthur Miller, but all her marriages ended in divorce. She died alone, after taking sleeping tablets, in her Los Angeles flat on 5th August 1962, at the age of 36.

Charlie Chaplin (_____ – 1977) spent his early years in _____ . When he was five, he _____ . He later joined the Karno Company, a comedy group. In 1912 he left England and moved to _____ . He was soon working as an actor and director, and he made _____ short films in 1914. By 1916 he was getting $_____ a week. His first long film was *The Kid*, which was made in _____ . *City Lights* came out in _____ and _____ came out in 1936. Chaplin continued to make silent films until 1940. In 1952 he left America and went to live in _____ . He received _____ in 1972. _____ on Christmas Day, 1977.

✂ -

B

Charlie Chaplin was born in 1889 and he grew up in London, where his family was very poor. He first went on the stage at the age of five and by the time he was 17 he was working with a comedy group called the Karno Company. When they went on tour in the USA in 1912, Charlie decided to stay there. He appeared in his first film in 1914.

In that year he made 35 short silent comedy films as actor and director. This was also the year when he created his most famous character, 'the Tramp'. By 1916 his weekly pay was $10,000 and he was world famous. His first long film, *The Kid* (1921), was a huge success. Other great films, like *The Gold Rush* (1925), *City Lights* (1931) and *Modern Times* (1936), were even more popular. In 1928 sound was introduced to films and studios started making 'talking pictures', but Chaplin continued to make silent films until 1940.

Later Chaplin was attacked for his political opinions. He left the USA in 1952 to make his home in Switzerland. He returned to America only once, 20 years later, to receive a special Oscar for his life's work. He died in his Swiss home on 25th December 1977, at the age of 88.

Marilyn Monroe's real name was _____ . She was born in _____ in Los Angeles. She had a job in a _____ before she started working as a model in 1944. Her first film was in 1947. _____ was the year when she became a big Hollywood star – she made _____ films in that year. But her most popular film was _____ , which came out in _____ . She married _____ times. One of her husbands, Joe DiMaggio, was a famous _____ player and Arthur Miller was a _____ . Marilyn was only _____ years old when she died in _____ in 1962.

Hall of fame

Language focus
should; mixed tenses;
comparative and
superlative adjectives

Key vocabulary
language connected with
fame and achievement

Skills focus
writing and speaking:
expressing opinions and
giving reasons

Level
upper-intermediate

Time
35–45 minutes

Preparation
one photocopy for each
student

Extra notes
It is a good idea (but
not essential) to hand
out the worksheets
before the lesson so
that students have
time to find or check
information about
people in the lists.

Warm-up

❶ Explain or elicit the meaning of *Hall of Fame* (a place that provides a memorial for famous people and their achievements).

❷ Ask students to think about a *Hall of Fame* for people from their country. Brainstorm names for each of the four categories on the worksheet and write them on the board.

Main activity

❶ Hand out the worksheets and ask students to identify the people in the photos 1 *Venus Williams*, 2 *Justin Timberlake*, 3 *Johnny Depp*, 4 *Princess Diana*.

❷ Ask students to imagine that they are organising a Hall of Fame for the most famous people of the past 50 years. Working individually, they rank the names in each category in order of importance.

❸ Divide the class into groups of four students and explain the situation for the activity: *Your group is setting up a Hall of Fame. Unfortunately, money is limited and you can only include a few people from this list.* Explain that they need to choose two people from each of the four categories. Their choices should include both women and men.

❹ Groups discuss each category and decide on two names. If they cannot reach agreement through discussion, they should take a vote. If the vote is tied, they should toss a coin. Set a time limit of about ten minutes for this discussion.

❺ Each group member takes charge of one category and writes a paragraph explaining why the two people were chosen and why others were rejected.

❻ Students read each other's paragraphs and suggest improvements if necessary.

❼ Ask students to read out their paragraphs to the class. Write the selected names on the board. Where there is disagreement, invite class discussion.

Follow-up

◯ Ask students to watch the news, read a newspaper or look at a news website on a specified day. They should list the famous people who appear and write two sentences in English about each one. In the next lesson, they share their information.

◯ Students choose one person from the Warm-up and write a paragraph explaining why he/she should be Number 1 in their country's *Hall of Fame*. If they do this for homework, students could be asked to include a photo of the person they write about.

1

Sports heroes

Michael Jordan ☐
Lance Armstrong ☐
David Beckham ☐
Carolina Klüft ☐
Venus Williams ☐
Cristiano Ronaldo ☐
Tiger Woods ☐

2

Musicians

Paul McCartney ☐
Madonna ☐
Bob Marley ☐
Britney Spears ☐
Elvis Presley ☐
Justin Timberlake ☐
Beyonce Knowles ☐

3

Actors

Keira Knightley ☐
Leonardo diCaprio ☐
Tom Hanks ☐
Nicole Kidman ☐
Angelina Jolie ☐
Johnny Depp ☐
Will Smith ☐

4

Others

Princess Diana ☐
Bill Gates ☐
Pablo Picasso ☐
J.K. Rowling ☐
Oprah Winfrey ☐
Stephen Spielberg ☐
Nelson Mandela ☐

Guess my job

Language focus
present simple questions

Key vocabulary
jobs and the workplace

Skills focus
speaking: asking for information; making deductions

Level
elementary

Time
25–30 minutes

Preparation
one photocopy for each group of 4 to 6 students, cut into separate cards

Extra notes
You may want to discard cards with unknown words on them.

Warm-up

❶ Write these phrases on the board: *wear a uniform, work inside, work outside*. Make sure that students understand the meaning of each one.

❷ Divide the class into groups of four to six. Each group must think of three jobs that fit with each phrase on the board, e.g. a *police officer* wears a uniform. The first group to finish wins. Some of the groups read out their answers to the class.

Main activity

❶ Hand out a set of cards to each group, to be placed face down on the table.

❷ Explain to students that they are going to play a game where they ask questions to guess people's jobs. They can only use questions that can be answered *Yes* or *No* and they are allowed a maximum of 15 questions.

❸ Demonstrate by asking a student to pick up a card without showing anyone. Invite the rest of the class to ask this student *yes/no* questions to find out what the job is. Ask some questions yourself. Examples:
Do you usually work inside/outside?
Do you wear a uniform / special clothes?
Do you work alone / in an office / in a shop?
Are you good at maths/science/art/sport?
Is your job dangerous?

❹ Students play the game in their groups. They take it in turns to pick up a card and the others ask questions. Whoever guesses the job keeps the card. If no one gets the answer after 15 questions, the cardholder gives the answer and keeps the card.

❺ Call 'Time's up!' after about 15 minutes. The person with the most cards at the end is the winner.

Follow-up

○ Ask students in pairs to choose a job and write about a day in the life of someone who does that job. They can find out information about the job on the Internet and add interesting facts and relevant pictures.

○ Students do some research about a job they are interested in. Then they write a list of five things they like about that job and five things they don't, without putting the job title at the top. They exchange lists with a partner and try to guess each other's jobs.

nurse	footballer	writer	police officer
doctor	mechanic	artist	soldier
teacher	actor/actress	photographer	hairdresser
cleaner	secretary	model	waiter/waitress
farmer	taxi driver	builder	dentist
baker	pilot	gardener	chef
shop assistant	bus driver	pop star	fire fighter

Job interviews

Language focus
mixed tenses

Key vocabulary
*applicant,
communication,
enthusiastic,
environment, interviewer,
opportunity, rewarding,
serve, strength, weakness*

Skills focus
reading and speaking:
responding to a job
advert; doing a job
interview

Level
intermediate

Time
45–50 minutes

Preparation
one photocopy for each
student

Extra notes
If possible, write the
Warm-up questions on
the board before the
lesson to save time.

Warm-up

❶ Ask students if there is anyone who has had an interview for a job. If some answer yes, ask them to describe the experience.

❷ Write some or all of the following questions on the board:
Tell us about yourself. Do you have any experience in this sort of work? Why do you think you would be good at this job? How would your teachers describe you? What are your strengths and weaknesses? Do you like working as part of a team?
Tell students: *These are some of the questions that you could be asked in an interview for your first job.* Discuss with the class what the interviewer wants to find out, and elicit both good and bad answers.

Main activity

❶ Hand out the worksheets. Explain that the text at the top is a job advertisement from a job search website. Read it with the class and check comprehension.

❷ Put students in pairs. Tell them that they are going to prepare for interviews for the job at Romano's restaurant.

❸ Ask pairs to look at the *Interviewers* box and discuss the *Before the interviews* questions. Ask them to write eight questions as interviewers for the job. They can use some questions from the Warm-up, but should also add others. If necessary, you can help with ideas for extra questions, e.g. *What do customers want when they go to a restaurant? What makes a good waiter or waitress? How well do you work under pressure? Can you work at night/weekends?* Set a time limit of 10–15 minutes for this step.

❹ Now ask students to work on their own. Give them about five minutes to look at the *Applicants* box and prepare some things to say in the role of applicant for the job at Romano's. They should use true information about themselves.

❺ Put pairs together to make groups of four for the first role play. Pair A takes the role of interviewers for the job and they interview the two applicants from pair B, one after the other. Tell them to take it in turns to ask their questions, and to make brief notes on their worksheet. While one applicant in pair B is being interviewed, the other can listen but must not speak.

❻ After the first set of interviews, pairs discuss the *After the interviews* questions on their worksheet.

❼ Students swap roles and work in new groups of four for the second set of interviews. B students now take the role of the interviewers and A students take the role of applicants.

❽ When students have completed the interviews, invite general feedback from the class. Which questions were easy/difficult to answer? How did they handle the difficult questions? How could they improve?

Follow-up

○ Ask students to write an email to a friend after their job interview. Encourage them to describe their experience and talk about how well they performed.

○ Ask pairs to practise a comical version of a job interview, where everything goes wrong. They should use the interview questions they wrote in step 3 of the activity and prepare some terrible answers that are *not* what the employer wants to hear. Ask some pairs to act out their interview for the class.

Job title:	Waiter/Waitress
Minimum age:	16 years old
Job type:	Full-time or part-time

If you are looking for a rewarding job, you have found the right place with **Romano's**! You will have the opportunity to work with other team members serving great food in a friendly environment.

We are looking for friendly, enthusiastic people who enjoy serving customers. Applicants need to have good communication skills and must be able to work well as part of a team.

We will teach you everything you need to know.

Interviewers

Before the interviews
What sort of person are you looking for?
What <u>don't</u> you want?

What questions can you ask to find the right person?
1 ....
2 ....
3 ....
4 ....
5 ....
6 ....
7 ....
8 ....

During the interviews – notes
....
....
....

After the interviews – discussion
What were the applicants' strengths and weaknesses in the interviews?

Applicants

Before the interview
What do you think this employer wants?
What questions can you expect? How will you answer them?
What questions would you like to ask?

After the interview – discussion
How did you do? Did you show your strengths?
Were there some questions that you could have answered better?
Do you think you would get this job?

My ideal job

Language focus
present simple questions;
gerunds; *would*

Key vocabulary
jobs and qualities;
*ambitious, colleague,
creative, deadline, earn,
easy-going, leader,
machinery, mend,
perform, practical,
responsibility, self-
employed, solve,
technology*

Skills focus
writing and speaking:
completing a
questionnaire;
identifying personal
attributes and skills

Level
upper-intermediate

Time
25–35 minutes

Preparation
one photocopy for each
student

Extra notes
Dictionaries may
be useful for this
activity. This activity
is particularly useful
with students who
are preparing to leave
school.

Warm-up

❶ Put the following headings on the board: *wearing a uniform, working in an office, working outside*. Ask the class to give you two jobs that fit under each heading, e.g. *police officer/soldier; secretary/company director; footballer/farmer; waiter/baker*.

❷ Brainstorm names of jobs and make a list on the board. Make the list as long as possible. Leave the list on the board for reference.

Main activity

❶ Explain to students that they are going to find their *ideal job*. Hand out the questionnaires. You may want to distribute dictionaries at this point. Ask them to complete the questionnaire with true answers. They must not show each other their answers. Set a time limit of ten minutes.

❷ Students turn over their questionnaires and write their name and a job they would like to do on the back. This information must be kept hidden. Collect all the papers in.

❸ Divide the class into pairs. Redistribute the completed questionnaires, giving two to each pair. Make sure they do not look on the back. The identity of the student who filled them in must be kept secret.

❹ In pairs, students discuss the two completed questionnaires they have received. They have to agree on three suitable jobs for each person and write them on the paper. They can refer to the list of jobs on the board or suggest other ones. They should look at all three sections to make sure the job fits. For example, if they suggest *teacher*, the person should have ticked *working with children* and selected *enjoying your job* but should not have ticked *quiet*!

❺ When they have completed the task, invite them to report back to the class. Ask some pairs to name one of the jobs they wrote down, e.g. *teacher*. The others ask questions to check this choice of job, e.g. *Does he or she like helping people? Does he or she like working in a team? Is he or she patient?*

❻ Finally, allow students to turn the questionnaire over and find out whose it is. Did their suggestions match the student's own choice of job? Return the questionnaires to their owners so they can see their *ideal jobs*!

Follow-up

○ Students write a *personal statement* about themselves to prepare for a job interview. They should write about what they are good at, what they are interested in and why they want to do the job.

○ Ask students to find an advertisement for a job on the Internet. They then decide which four adjectives from the questionnaire are most important for that job.

1 What would you look for in a job? Tick the boxes.

- [ ] using new technology
- [ ] helping people
- [ ] using machinery
- [ ] working with children
- [ ] doing sports
- [ ] explaining things
- [ ] being self-employed
- [ ] performing on stage
- [ ] being outside

- [ ] working in an office
- [ ] giving new ideas
- [ ] being a leader
- [ ] using your hands
- [ ] working with animals
- [ ] solving problems
- [ ] mending things
- [ ] having responsibility
- [ ] wearing a uniform

2 What is more important for you? Circle your choice.
1 working in a team / working on your own
2 good colleagues / a nice place to work in
3 enjoying your job / earning a lot of money
4 working to deadlines / taking as much time as you need
5 working near home / opportunity to travel

3 Tick the three adjectives that describe you best.

ambitious	[ ]	polite	[ ]
careful	[ ]	quick-thinking	[ ]
creative	[ ]	practical	[ ]
friendly	[ ]	kind	[ ]
hard-working	[ ]	confident	[ ]
intelligent	[ ]	quiet	[ ]
patient	[ ]	easy-going	[ ]

Past history

Language focus
Wh- questions; past simple

Key vocabulary
ancient, artist, come down, cut off, die, director, leader, marry, moon, paint, president, star, take place, wall

Skills focus
reading and speaking: answering quiz questions

Level
elementary

Time
30–35 minutes

Preparation
one photocopy for each group of 3 or 4 students, cut into separate cards; a photocopy of the Rules for each group (optional)

Warm-up

❶ Revise past simple questions with a noughts and crosses game. Draw a grid of nine squares on the board and write a past tense verb in each square (e.g. *played, painted, wrote, made, was*, etc.). Divide the class into two teams, 0 and X.

❷ In turn, a member of each team chooses a verb and uses it to make a question in the past simple (e.g. *Did you play hockey last weekend? Who painted this picture? When did she write the email?*). If the question is grammatically correct, rub out the verb and write either 0 or X in the square. If there is a mistake in the question, the verb remains in its square and can be used again. A team wins the game if they can get three 0s or three Xs in a row, horizontally, vertically or diagonally.

❸ Play the game again with different verbs.

Main activity

❶ Divide the class into groups of three or four students. Seat each group at a table.

❷ Hand out the cards and tell students to put them face down on the table.

❸ Tell students that they are going to play a quiz game about people and events in the past. Ask for a volunteer in each group to keep the scores.

❹ Explain the rules of the game – see the Rules box below.

❺ Set a time limit of 15 minutes for students to play the game. If any group finishes early, they can continue by making up their own past tense quiz questions.

❻ With the whole class, pick out a few of the questions in the quiz and ask students to say more about the person or event.

Follow-up

⭘ Find a suitable online quiz on the past tense in English (there are many of these available on the Internet – type in *past simple quiz* or *past simple test* on your search engine). Give students the website address and ask them to do the quiz for homework. Check their scores in the next lesson.

⭘ Make a class quiz about the school. Brainstorm to elicit questions in the present and past simple, and write all suggestions on the board. Work with the class to select a set of 20 questions and ask students to write them down in a list. Give these lists to another English teacher to use as a quiz in his/her class. In the next lesson, hand back the answers for your students to mark and then return them to the other class.

Rules for Past history

1 If you are the first player (A), pick up a card and read out the question for player B on your left. Do not let the others see the card. If B can answer the question correctly, he/she gets two points.

2 If the answer is wrong, the other players take it in turns to answer. If someone answers the question correctly, they get 1 point.

3 Then it is player B's turn to pick up a card and ask a question for player C.

4 The game continues like this until all the cards are used. The player with the most points at the end is the winner.

✂

Who wrote *Romeo and Juliet* and *Hamlet*? [William Shakespeare]	**What country did Cleopatra come from?** [Egypt]	**Who was the President of the USA from 2001 to 2009?** [George W. Bush]
Which French leader was married to Josephine? [Napoleon]	**Which James Bond film starred Daniel Craig in 2006?** [*Casino Royale*]	**Which team won the football World Cup in 2006?** [Italy]
When did World War II end? [1945]	**Who wrote the opera *The Marriage of Figaro*?** [Mozart]	**Who married one of the Spice Girls in 1999?** [David Beckham]
Ringo Starr was a member of The Beatles. What instrument did he play? [the drums]	**Who painted the *Mona Lisa*?** [Leonardo da Vinci]	**Where did the first Olympic Games take place?** [Greece (Olympia)]
What was the nationality of Ludwig van Beethoven? [German]	**When did men first walk on the moon?** [1969]	**Who wrote the Harry Potter books?** [J.K. Rowling]
When did the Berlin Wall come down? [1989]	**Which sport did Justine Henin play?** [tennis]	**Which actress played Elizabeth Swann in the *Pirates of the Caribbean* films?** [Keira Knightley]
Which famous artist cut off part of his ear? [Vincent van Gogh]	**Who was the director of the *Star Wars* films?** [George Lucas]	**Where did Julius Caesar die?** [in Rome]
Who recorded the song *Umbrella* in 2007? [Rihanna]	**Where were the *Lord of the Rings* films made?** [New Zealand]	**In the ancient Greek story, who was the most beautiful woman in the world?** [Helen]

School reunion

Language focus
past simple; present
perfect; present
continuous

Key vocabulary
*architect, assistant,
champion, chef,
community, court,
designer, environment,
exhibition, homeless,
jewellery, lawyer,
necklace, presenter, share,
soap opera, social worker,
talent competition, vet*

Skills focus
reading and speaking:
describing past events
and experiences;
describing present
activities

Level
intermediate

Time
40–45 minutes

Preparation
one or two photocopies
of both worksheets
(pages 101 and 102), cut
into separate cards

Extra notes
Dictionaries may be
useful for this activity.

Warm-up

❶ Explain the meaning of *school reunion* (an occasion when ex-students come back to their old school to meet each other). Ask students if they think this is a good idea and to say why or why not.

❷ Ask students to imagine coming back to the school for a reunion with their classmates. What would they say? What would they want to find out? Elicit examples of greetings and questions, for example:
Hello! How are you?
Hey! I remember you!
You look great / just the same / different!
What are you doing now?
Do you still (live/like/play …)?
What did you do when/after …?
Did you go to university?
Are you married?
This is (name) – do you remember him/her?

Main activity

❶ For a class of 16 students or less, the role play should be a whole class activity. For a larger number, divide the class into two halves for two separate role plays, using a duplicate set of role cards. Give one card to each student. There may be some cards that you don't need to use.

❷ Explain the situation for the role play. Tell students that they are going to meet their classmates for the first time in ten years at a school reunion.

❸ Ask them to read their role card about their life in the past ten years. If there is anything they don't understand, they should ask you or use a dictionary. Ask them to think of other information and details they can add.

❹ Either as a whole class or in their groups, students mingle and exchange information. They can take their card with them to refer to if necessary, but encourage them to speak without looking at it and to express themselves in their own words. Set a time limit of 20–25 minutes.

❺ After the role play, ask students to describe some of the interesting things they heard. If they need prompting, you can ask: *Who was the happiest / most successful person you met? Who had the most important / most enjoyable / most unusual / most difficult job?*

Follow-up

○ Ask students to write an email to a friend describing the experience of going to the school reunion.

○ Make copies of both pages of role cards, one set for each pair, and hand them out for students to read. Ask pairs to discuss which person they would most like to be and who they *wouldn't* like to be, and why. Then discuss with the whole class.

You studied at university for five years and then became a vet.

At first you lived and worked in the city – you were usually looking after people's pets.

You wanted to work with farm animals, so you moved to the country last year. You're the only vet in the village where you live.

You've been married for six months.

After school you travelled round the world for two years. You worked in part-time jobs in Canada and New Zealand.

When you came back, you worked as a kitchen assistant in a restaurant.

On the job, you started learning how to cook and now you're a good chef.

You met your husband/wife four years ago. You have two young children.

When you were 19 you were on TV as a singer in a talent competition.

You started a band and sang in clubs and at parties. The band broke up after two years.

You took dance lessons and you've been on stage in musicals. You're appearing in a new musical next week.

You love your work, but it's hard to make good money.

You share a flat with two other musicians.

You've always been good at art and you're interested in computers.

In your first job you designed adverts for magazines.

Now you're a website designer and you enjoy this work.

Your hobby is flying – you learnt to fly a plane five years ago.

You bought a flat last year.

Your dream was to be a swimming champion. You trained hard and you were in the national team when you were 19.

You won two gold medals in international competitions.

Later you became a radio presenter for a sports programme. You met lots of great sports stars.

Four months ago the programme ended and at the moment you aren't working.

You used to be a police officer but you didn't enjoy this work.

You studied part-time and became a social worker.

For two years you had a job giving help to homeless people. You enjoyed the work, although it was difficult.

Now you're managing a youth centre where young people can get help and advice.

You're going to get married next year.

You started work as a house painter.

You borrowed money to buy your first house seven years ago.

Since then you've bought and sold houses and flats and you've made a lot of money.

You live in a big house near the sea.

You met your husband/wife on a skiing holiday four years ago. You've got a new baby who is six weeks old.

After school you studied music for four years. You're very good at playing the piano and the keyboard.

You taught music in a school but you left this job after a few years.

You started writing music and this has been a success. Well-known musicians have recorded some of your songs.

You live in a small flat in a quiet part of the city.

After school you studied computer science at university. Your first job was testing computer games for a big company.

Two years ago you became a game designer in the company.

Last year you started your own business with two friends. You've got lots of ideas for new computer games.

You share a flat with a friend in the city centre.

You got married when you were very young.

You used to draw pictures for your two children.

A friend was writing a children's book and asked you to draw the pictures. The book won a prize and was very popular.

Now you're a successful artist. You had an exhibition of paintings in a gallery last month.

You work at home in a small town.

While you were studying at college, you worked for a student radio station.

You became a news reporter for a TV channel.

You've travelled abroad many times and you've been in some dangerous situations.

You're often away from home and you have to work long hours.

You're married with one child.

You've lived in lots of different places and had lots of jobs.

Six years ago you started collecting old jewellery. Your best buy was a necklace – you bought it for £15 and sold it last year for £8,000.

Now you have your own shop. You also buy and sell jewellery on the Internet.

You often go abroad to look for interesting jewellery in unusual places.

After school you studied at university and became an architect.

You started working for a big company which builds cheap houses.

You wanted to design better buildings that would help the environment.

Three years ago you designed a low-energy office building which won several prizes.

You designed your own flat in the city centre.

After school you took a drama course and trained to be an actor.

At first it was difficult to find work and you were very poor.

In the past three years you've had some good parts in TV dramas and soap operas.

You worked in the USA for a year.

You aren't interested in marriage or children at the moment.

You studied for six years and became a lawyer four years ago.

Your career has been very successful. You've helped several famous people in court. Your wife/husband is also a lawyer. You haven't got any children.

You live in a large house and you're planning to buy a second home in France.

You've always wanted to help people so you decided to become a nurse.

You got a job in a hospital in a small town.

Now you're a community nurse – you visit people in their homes.

The pay isn't very good, but you love the work. You know most people in the town and you've got lots of friends.

You aren't married, but you've recently met someone nice.

Mixed stories

Language focus
past simple; past continuous; past perfect

Key vocabulary
amazement, collector, (luggage) compartment, disappointed, for sale, game warden, illegal, notice, owner, passenger permission, proud, truthful

Skills focus
reading and speaking: sequencing two stories; devising endings

Level
upper-intermediate

Time
40 minutes

Preparation
one photocopy of both worksheets (pages 104 and 105) for each pair, cut up into separate parts

Extra notes
Dictionaries may be useful for this activity. For a shorter and simpler version of the activity, you can hand out one story only for pairs to work on.

Warm-up

❶ Write the following words as a list on the board: *When, While, Although, Then, After that, After a while, However, Suddenly, Immediately, Finally.*

❷ Build up a class story as a 'chain' activity. Start off by giving the students an opening sentence, e.g. *I was getting ready for school on Monday morning when suddenly my phone rang.* Ask a student to follow with a second sentence, then nominate others to continue in turn, each adding a sentence. From time to time, when appropriate, point to one of the words on the board. The next student must start his/her sentence with the word you have indicated.

❸ Keep the story going for as long as possible and try to reach a satisfactory ending.

Main activity

❶ Pre-teach the expression *game warden* (*game* here means wild animals that are hunted; a game warden is responsible for making sure that hunting rules are obeyed). You might also decide to pre-teach other words, e.g. *collector, compartment, passenger* – but if there are similar words in the students' language, you may prefer to let them work out the meanings for themselves. Alternatively, you may want to hand out dictionaries.

❷ Put students in pairs and hand out the sentence parts, thoroughly mixed in a random order.

❸ Explain that the sentence parts make up two separate stories. Students need to work with their partner to sort out the parts for each story and put them in the right order. Tell them to find the two story openings as a first step.

❹ Explain that the stories have been left incomplete at the end. Ask pairs to try to predict the ending for each story and to write down their suggestions.

❺ Set a time limit of 20 minutes to complete the activity. If some pairs finish early, they can go round and help slower ones.

❻ Choose students to read the completed stories aloud while the others check. Then invite other pairs to read out their suggestions for the two endings. Finally, tell them the original endings:

Text 1: 'I'm the biggest damn liar in the whole United States.'
Text 2: 'The violin is yours, Mr Kreisler. Take it into the world, and let people hear it.'

Follow-up

○ Ask students to rewrite one of the stories from the viewpoint of the secondary character: either the game warden or the collector.

○ Ask pairs to practise retelling one or other of the stories in their own words, without looking at the original version. Then choose a pair to tell each story to the class. If they get stuck or go wrong, the others can help them out.

(15.3) Mixed stories

The American writer Mark Twain, who wrote the book *Huckleberry Finn*, used to love fishing

and was very proud of his skills. He once spent three weeks catching fish

in the forest in Maine, although the fishing season had already

closed and fishing was illegal. When he got on the train at the end of this time, he was

feeling very pleased with himself. His fish were in a box of ice

in the luggage compartment, and now he was sitting comfortably in his

seat, ready for the journey home. As the train travelled along, he started a

conversation with another passenger in his compartment and soon he was

telling this man all about his successes on the river. After a while he

noticed that the other passenger was not smiling. 'By the way, who are you, sir?'

he asked. 'I'm the state game warden,' was the unwelcome reply. 'Who

are you?' Twain opened his eyes wide. 'Well, to be perfectly truthful, warden,'

he said, 'I'm …

Fritz Kreisler, born in Austria, was one of the best-known musicians of his time and

made many classical recordings. When he was still a young man, he was

looking around in a shop one day when he found a wonderful violin that he

wanted to buy. But at that time he didn't have much money. By the time he had

got enough and returned to buy the instrument, he discovered that it

had already been sold to a collector. He went to the new

owner's home and asked him if he would sell it. But

the collector replied that this violin was important to him and it wasn't

for sale. Disappointed, Kreisler turned away – but before he left,

he asked if he could play it once more before it was put back in the collector's

cupboard. The man agreed and Kreisler began to play. The violin produced music of

such beauty that the collector could only listen in amazement. 'I have no right to

keep that to myself,' he said afterwards. 'The violin …

What are you doing?

Language focus
is/are; present continuous

Key vocabulary
boots, camp, dining room, fire, map, mountain, newspaper, postcard, shorts, ski, smile, snow, surf, tent, waiter, windy

Skills focus
speaking: talking on the phone; describing places and present activities

Level
elementary

Time
25–30 minutes

Preparation
one photocopy for each pair, cut into A and B parts

Warm-up

❶ Ask students how often they call their friends on the phone and why they call.

❷ Ask them to think about being away on holiday. In a phone call to a friend, what would they want to say and what would they want to find out? Elicit some useful expressions, for example:
Greetings: *Hi/Hello (name). This is (name). / It's (name) here.*
Questions: *Where are you? What are you doing? What's the place/hotel/weather like?*
Responding: *Really? Wow! That sounds great/awful. What about you?*
Checking: *What was that? I didn't catch that. What did you say?*
Ending: *I have to go now. I'll call you later/tomorrow. See you soon.*

Main activity

❶ Put students in pairs and hand out an A and a B worksheet to each pair. Students must not look at their partner's worksheet.

❷ Ask students to imagine that they are the person on the phone in their picture. Explain that they are both away on holiday with their family and they are going to talk to each other on the phone about what is happening. Ask them to talk about where they are, what the weather is like, what they and the other members of their family are doing and whether or not they are having a good time. Point out that there are other family members visible in the picture.

❸ Give students a few minutes to look at their picture and think about what they will say. Remind them to use the present continuous for things that are happening now. Encourage them to make the phone call interactive by asking each other plenty of questions.

❹ Seat pairs back to back, so that they can hear but not see each other during the phone conversation. Tell student A to make the call and start the conversation. Set a time limit of five minutes.

❺ At the end of the call, students turn back to face each other. They report back to their partner all that they can remember about what they heard, using the present continuous (e.g. *You're in the mountains in France and you're having breakfast in the hotel …*). Their partner corrects the information if necessary.

❻ Now ask students to look at each other's pictures. Is the scene how they imagined it from the phone conversation?

❼ With the whole class, ask students to say which holiday they would prefer and why.

Follow-up

◯ Ask students to write a paragraph comparing the two pictures, using *is/are* and the present continuous.

◯ Put students in pairs and ask them to imagine what happened in each place after the phone call. What did the people do next? After discussion, students report their ideas to the class, using the past simple.

A

Meribel, France, 9.00 am

B

Byron Bay, Australia, 6.00 pm

Ask the question

Language focus
Wh- questions; mixed tenses

Key vocabulary
forest, Greek, the Nile, penguin, Portuguese, Roman, twice

Skills focus
speaking: asking questions

Level
intermediate

Time
40 minutes

Preparation
one photocopy for each pair, cut into A and B parts

Warm-up

❶ Ask one student to think of an object in their home, without saying the word aloud. Invite the others to ask questions to guess what the object is. Examples: *Is it big / small / useful / a machine / a piece of furniture? Where is it? What do you do with it? What's it made of? What colour is it? How often do you use it?*

❷ Choose four other students to think of different things for the class to guess: a type of food, an animal, a person and a place. This will require students to think of some different questions from the examples above.

Main activity

❶ Tell students that you are going to give them a list of answers. Their aim will be to think of questions they can ask to produce these exact answers.

❷ Give them an example: write *A volcano* on the board. Elicit questions that will produce this answer, e.g. *What is Mount Etna? What was Krakatoa? What kind of mountain sometimes erupts / explodes / produces fire and smoke?* You could do the same with a second example, e.g. *In the spring. (When do trees turn green after the winter? When do we see lots of flowers after the winter? When do birds usually build their nests?)*

❸ Put students in pairs and hand out an A and a B worksheet to each pair. Students must not look at their partner's worksheet.

❹ Give them five minutes to read their list of answers and think of questions they can ask. They must do this on their own. Stress that the questions they ask must be designed to elicit the exact answers they have on their worksheet.

❺ Set a time limit of six to eight minutes. Student A asks questions to try to elicit the correct answers from student B. For each correct answer, A puts a tick in the second column of the table. If students don't get the exact answer they are looking for, they should try to think of a clearer question. If they are having trouble with a particular answer, they should move on and return to it later. Ensure they do not look at their partner's worksheet.

❻ When time is up, call 'Stop!' Students change roles and B asks the questions.

❼ Find out who has the most ticks in their table. Choose some of the more difficult items in each table and ask students what questions they asked.

Follow-up

○ Ask students to write a list of six answers similar to those on the worksheet, and a separate list of questions to go with them. In pairs, they swap their answers and write down what they think their partner's questions are. Then they compare their lists of questions.

○ Write *Wh-* questions on labels and stick a label on each student's back. Example questions: *Who is your favourite singer? What do you have for breakfast? When did you get up this morning? What kind of computer have you got?* Students mingle, read each other's questions and answer them. On the basis of the answers they get, they have to guess what question is written on their label. When they have guessed, they take off their label and continue to give answers to other students. Set a time limit of six to eight minutes for this activity.

B Answers

✓	
1 A forest.	
2 In the sea.	
3 Black.	
4 Shakespeare.	
5 Thirsty.	
6 Yes, she did.	
7 Twelve.	
8 Greek.	
9 Once a year.	
10 On Friday.	
11 No, I don't.	
12 Eggs.	
13 The Romans.	
14 Tomorrow.	
15 A knife.	

✂ -

A Answers

✓	
1 Portuguese.	
2 Harry Potter.	
3 Seven.	
4 Vegetables.	
5 Yes, it does.	
6 Tired.	
7 In the autumn.	
8 In Paris.	
9 Pink.	
10 Twice a day.	
11 The Nile.	
12 Yesterday.	
13 Penguins.	
14 Slowly.	
15 No, they didn't.	

Amazon

Language focus
modals: *can, should, must*; first conditional; *to* + infinitive of purpose

Key vocabulary
antibiotics, axe, bandage, battery, canoe, compass, frying pan, hammock, insect repellent, life jacket, raincoat, saucepan, tin (of food), vitamins

Skills focus
speaking: stating opinions; giving reasons; negotiating

Level
upper-intermediate

Time
35–40 minutes

Preparation
one photocopy for each student; dictionaries; a map of South America for the Warm-up (optional)

Warm-up

1 Ask students to say what they know about the Amazon rainforest, e.g.
Which continent is it in? (South America)
Which country has the largest area of rainforest? (Brazil)
Describe the vegetation. (tall trees, dense growth, a huge variety of plants)
What's the climate like? (warm, wet, humid).
If possible, use a map to show the Amazon River and its many tributaries.

2 Tell students that you would like to visit the Brazilian rainforest. What should you do beforehand? What clothes and other things should you take? Elicit some suggestions, for example: *You should book a hotel / read about the wildlife / organise a river tour. You should take light clothes / a raincoat / a camera.* Keep this brief and don't go into much detail.

Main activity

1 Hand out the worksheets.

2 Explain to students that their group is planning to make a journey of 600 km through the Brazilian rainforest. They are going to travel in canoes, sometimes on the Amazon River and sometimes on smaller rivers which are very remote. Now they are planning what to take with them. Space on the canoes is limited, so they need to reduce the list to just 20 items.

3 Ask students to read the list on their own and check the meaning of new words in a dictionary. Tell them to put a tick beside items they think are essential and a cross beside items they would definitely remove from the list.

4 Divide the class into groups of three or four students. In their groups, students make arguments to support their opinions and try to reach agreement through discussion. If they can't agree on all of the items after ten minutes, they should take a vote.

5 Ask each group to join up with another group to compare their decisions and discuss their reasons. While they are working, copy the list of items onto the board.

6 Ask one group to read out the items they decided to reject and invite others to comment. Where there is general agreement about an item, rub it off the board. Discuss areas of disagreement and try to arrive at a class consensus on the 20 most important items.

Follow-up

○ Ask students to write a diary entry describing a day on their canoe trip.

○ Tell students to choose one of these environments: *jungle, desert, alpine mountains.* Ask them to do some research on the Internet to find survival techniques that can help people stay alive in this environment. These could include tips on finding food/water, protecting yourself from heat/cold, making tools, building a shelter, making a fire, etc. Students compare their findings in the next lesson.

antibiotics
axe
bandages
batteries
bottled water
camera
chocolate
compass
dried food
fishing lines
frying pan
gun
hammocks
hats
insect repellent
knife
laptop computer
life jackets
map
matches
mirror
mobile phone
MP3 player
plastic bags
Portuguese dictionary
raincoats
rope
saucepan
sleeping bags
sun cream
tent
tin opener
tinned food
torch
two-way radio
vitamins

Plans and predictions

Language focus
will for predictions;
going to for plans

Key vocabulary
abroad, celebration, chat, competition, get married, one day, pass an exam, space, successful

Skills focus
speaking: asking and answering questions about the future

Level
elementary

Time
30 minutes

Preparation
one photocopy for 2 students, cut into A and B parts; mix up the 2 sets of photocopies so you can distribute them randomly

Warm-up

❶ Ask some questions about students' plans, e.g. *What are you going to do after school / have for lunch / do in your next lesson? Are you going to have an art lesson today / use your computer this evening / make any phone calls later?*

❷ Now tell students to look into the future and make predictions about what will happen. Prompt them by naming celebrities or events in the news to elicit sentences with *will*, e.g. *(Name) will be the next President. (Football team) will win the Champions League / World Cup. (Singer) will have a number one hit soon.* Follow up with *will* questions as appropriate.

Main activity

❶ Hand out the worksheets. Half the students should have the A version and the others should have the B version.

❷ You may need to pre-teach some words from the worksheets, e.g. *celebration, chat, one day, successful.*

❸ Explain that the aim of the activity is to find a name to write in every box in the second column. Students need to go round the class asking questions with *Will you …?* or *Are you going to …?* When they find someone who fits the description, they write the person's name in the second column. Encourage them to ask one or two more questions to get extra information for the third column.

❹ Give students a few minutes to read through their worksheet and think about their own answers.

❺ Students mingle, asking and answering. Because there are two worksheets, they will sometimes be answering on matters they have thought about, while at other times they will have to respond to questions they won't be expecting. Set a time limit of 15 minutes for the activity.

❻ Ask students to report back some interesting information that they received from people they spoke to.

Follow-up

⭕ Ask students to write two paragraphs, one on their short-term plans and the other on their long-term predictions about their life in the future. They can use topics from the worksheets or they can think of their own.

⭕ Ask students what they think *you* are going to do after school this afternoon, this evening and next weekend. Students discuss this in pairs and then offer their ideas, using *going to.* At the end, tell them what your plans actually are. Give a round of applause to the pair whose suggestions were the closest to being correct.

17.1 Plans and predictions

A

Find someone who ...	Name	Extra information
1 thinks they will pass all their exams this year.		
2 is going to send a text message after school today.		
3 thinks they will travel a lot in the future.		
4 isn't going to watch television this evening.		
5 is going to buy a present for someone soon.		
6 doesn't think they will get married before they are 26.		
7 thinks English will be useful to them in the future.		
8 is going to chat with friends on the Internet this evening.		
9 is going to be in a sports competition soon.		
10 doesn't think they will ever travel into space.		
11 is going to try to get a job in the summer holidays.		
12 thinks they will be famous one day.		

✂ -

B

Find someone who ...	Name	Extra information
1 is going to send an email to someone this evening.		
2 thinks they will work as a scientist or a doctor in the future.		
3 doesn't think they will study at university.		
4 is going to buy some new clothes at the weekend.		
5 thinks they will have more than two children.		
6 isn't going to travel by bus today.		
7 is going to have a music lesson tomorrow.		
8 doesn't think they will live abroad in the future.		
9 is going to visit a friend this afternoon.		
10 thinks their favourite sports team will be successful this year.		
11 is going to have a family celebration in the next month.		
12 thinks they will live to be 100.		

Life changes

Language focus
will and *going to* for predictions

Key vocabulary
personal information; future time expressions

Skills focus
writing and speaking: describing events and situations in the future

Level
intermediate

Time
45 minutes

Preparation
one photocopy for each pair; sheets of paper for the Warm-up

Warm-up

❶ Write the following sentence openings on the board:
My name is … (name)
In ten years' time I'm going to be a … (job)
I'll live in … (place)
I'll own a/an … (adjective + possession)
I'll … every day (activity)
I'll be … (adjective to describe a person)
Elicit possible endings.

❷ Hand out a sheet of paper to each student. They write the first sentence opening from the board at the top of their sheet, completing it with their name, then fold the paper over and pass it on to the next person. On the paper they receive, they write and complete the next sentence and again pass the paper on. When all six lines have been written like this, the paper is returned to the person named at the top. Ask students to read out the resulting description of their future.

Main activity

❶ Put students in pairs and hand out a worksheet to each pair.

❷ Explain that the central picture shows four young people as they are now, and the other pictures show them in 12 years' time. Students need to make up a story predicting what will happen to each person in this period.

❸ Take one person from the worksheet as an example. With the class, elicit suggestions and build up a paragraph of four or five sentences on the board about this person's life in the future. Include time expressions. For example:
When he leaves school he's going to …
Then / After that he will / he's going to …
Three years later / During the next three years he will …
The following year / In (year) / On (date) …

❹ In pairs, students look at the other three people in the pictures and make up stories about their future. After discussion, they write each story as a paragraph.

❺ Focus on each of the three people in turn and ask different pairs to read out their paragraph about him/her. Encourage others to ask questions and to comment on similarities and differences.

Follow-up

○ Ask students to find a photo of an interesting-looking person from a magazine or the Internet. Ask them to prepare a profile of this person's past, present and future. In the next lesson they show the photo and present their person to the class.

○ Ask students to write the story of one of the people on the worksheet as part of a biography, using past tenses.

Things to come

Language focus
will, *might*; future
perfect; future passive

Key vocabulary
*army, extinct, (polar) ice,
melt, population, space,
war*

Skills focus
speaking: predicting and
speculating about the
future

Level
upper-intermediate

Time
50 minutes

Preparation
one photocopy for each
group of 3 or 4 students,
cut into separate cards

Extra notes
For a shorter activity,
reduce the number of
cards you hand out.

Warm-up

❶ On the board, draw a simple picture of a car on a road. Brainstorm with the class words associated with this image and write them on the board. Examples might include *fast, expensive, freedom, pollution, shortage of oil, food miles, traffic jams, accidents*, etc.

❷ Ask students for their predictions on the subject of cars and driving in 25 years' time. Elicit sentences using different tenses, for example:
Petrol will be very expensive.
People will drive smaller cars.
We will have found a different type of fuel for cars.
Cars will be banned in the city centre.
Computers might control all the traffic on our roads.

Main activity

❶ Divide the class into groups of three or four students. Seat each group at a table.

❷ Hand out the cards and tell students to put them face down on the table. The cards can be in any order.

❸ When you call 'Go!' the first student takes a card and turns it over. The group has three minutes to respond to the image and to make predictions for 25 years' time. The student who turned over the card speaks first. Students will need to express their views quickly and concisely to fit into the time allowed.

❹ At the end of three minutes, call 'Stop!' Each group then has a few seconds to decide whether their views on this topic were *optimistic, pessimistic* or *undecided*. Ask them to write down the card number with *O, P* or *U* beside it.

❺ Now call 'Next card … go!' The second student takes the next card and starts the discussion. Continue in the same way until all the cards have been used.

❻ Go through the cards with the class, asking groups to say whether their views were optimistic, pessimistic or undecided. Where groups were undecided, or where there is marked disagreement between groups, open up the issue for class discussion.

Follow-up

○ Use two or more of the cards as the basis for group debates. Assign the same card to two different groups. One group prepares optimistic arguments and the other prepares pessimistic ones. Groups then debate the topic in front of the class. Give your comments at the end and encourage other students to give theirs.

○ Ask students to do some research on the Internet to find out more about one of the topics on the cards. They should aim to find at least three interesting facts. Tell them to use English-speaking websites where possible. In the next lesson, students share their information.

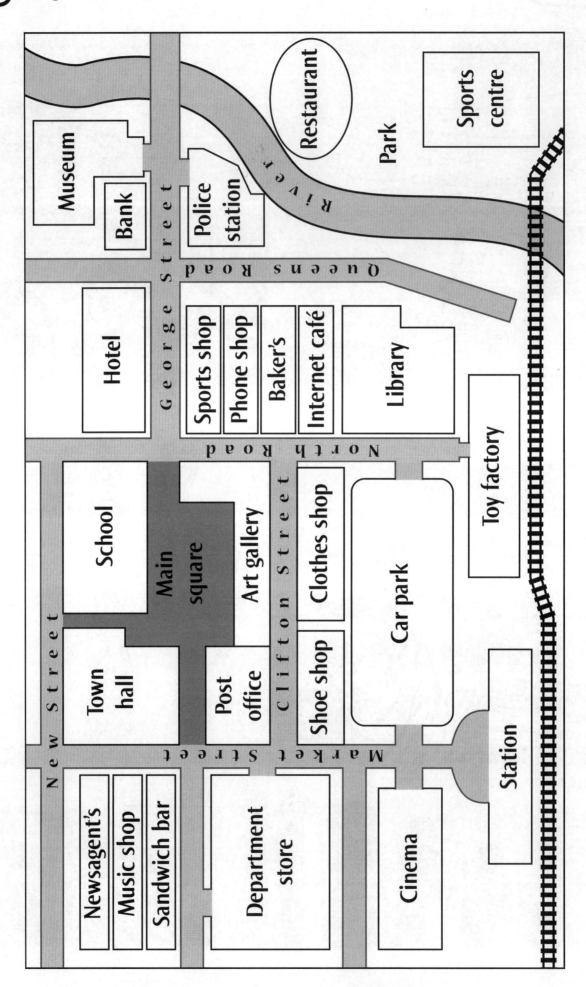

Thanks and acknowledgements

The authors would like to thank all the editors who have contributed to this project: Frances Amrani, Alison Silver and particularly Rosemary Bradley, who combined much needed patience and understanding with very helpful insights and suggestions. They would also like to thank Sara Bennett and James Dingle for their guidance during the initial stages of development.

Many thanks go to Cleo Ahn, Natasha Colbridge, Rosalia Valero-Elizondo, Derryl Fox, Merryn Grimley and Carolina Hernandez for all their help in piloting and reviewing material.

The publishers are grateful for permission to reproduce photographic material:

Alamy/Wolfgang Kaehler p111 (cl), Corbis/Cinema Photo p89 (br), Corbis/DLILLC p111 (br), Corbis/Lorenzo Ciniglio p91 (tl), Getty Images/Michael Ochs p89 (tr), Getty Images/National Geographic p111 (t), Getty Images/Richard Ross p19 (tl), Getty Images/Tim Graham p91 (br), Rex Features/Matt Baron/BEI p91 (tr) Rex Features/Theo Kingma p91 (bl), Shutterstock pp111 (bl), 19 (br), Still Pictures/ Mark Edwards p111 (cr).

The publishers are grateful to the following illustrators:

Kel Dyson pp21, 23, 33, 83, 115; Dylan Gibson pp25, 27, 53, 54, 81, 95, 97, 107, 117; Kamae Design pp13, 35, 39, 43, 87, 113, 118; Peter Kyprianou pp59, 71; Mark Watkinson pp29, 33, 47, 51, 67.

The publishers are also grateful to the following contributors:

Lucy Mordini: proofreading

Alison Prior: picture research services

Kamae Design Ltd: text design, layouts and some images